MYTHS ARE FUCKING GREAT

By

The Rt. Hon. Dr. Nemesis R. M. Lightslayer the Magnificent, Breaker of Spines and Tweaker of Unmentionables

ISBN: 978-1-291-97191-0

THIS BOOK IS FUCKING DEDICATED TO THE GODDESS MARY MOTHERFUCKING BEARD, AS WE BELIEVE WE MAY NOT HAVE SACRIFICED ENOUGH FUCKING VICTIMS TO HER AND WOULD RATHER AVOID UNNECESSARY SMITING. IN ADDITION TO THIS, DUTIFUL WORSHIP OF MARY MOTHERFUCKING BEARD HAS SAVED OUR LIVES MANY FUCKING TIMES, AND FOR THAT WE ARE EXTREMELY FUCKING GRATEFUL.

CONTENTS

GREEK MYTHOLOGY

THE ILIAD - 11
LET'S TALK ABOUT HERACLES - 28
HERACLES FUCKS SHIT UP - 30
THE LABOURS OF HERACLES - 31
HERACLES HAS KINKY FUN - 43
HERACLES GETS (ANOTHER) GIRL - 44
HERACLES FUCKS UP TROY - 45
A STORY ABOUT BUTTS - 46
TIRESIAS: THE SASSIEST MOTHERFUCKER IN THE MYTHOLOGICAL WORLD - 47
MOTHERFUCKING OEDIPUS - 48
ANTIGONE (A. K. A. MOTHERFUCKING OEDIPUS II) - 51
ATALANTA IS A BADASS MOTHERFUCKER WITH FRUIT PROBLEMS - 53
CAN WE JUST FUCKING TALK ABOUT PRIAPUS? - 54
APHRODITE - 55
MINOS HAS A BAD EXPERIENCE WITH A COW - 56
THESEUS JUST REALLY FUCKING HATES COWS - 57
DAEDALUS - 59
HIPPOLYTUS IS JUST REALLY FUCKING STUPID - 61
THE WORLD'S SHITTIEST WEDDING GIFT - 63
DOUBLE EGG SURPRISE - 64
HERA PLAYS THE GAME OF THRONES - 65
DEMETER GETS DOWN AND DIRTY - 66
SISTERS AGAINST INCEST - 67
PERSEUS - 68
ACHILLES IS ONE HOT LADY - 71
HERMES - 73
PARIS DEALS WITH AN EX - 75
PAN FUCKS EVERYTHING - 76
ACHILLES GETS HEARTBROKEN (AGAIN) - 77
ARION - 78
ATHENA GETS DIRTY - 79
WHEN SKINNY-DIPPING GOES WRONG - 80
MORE CHILD-EATING - 81

LETO - 82
SISYPHUS IS A COMPLETE ASSHOLE - 83
HUNGRY HUNGRY HIPPO - 85
HECATE - 86

ROMAN MYTHOLOGY

[ROME INTENSIFIES] - 89
ROMANS ARE DICKS - 90
HOLY FLYING DICK, BATMAN! - 91
CRAZY OLD LADY BURNS BOOKS - 92

EGYPTIAN MYTHOLOGY

BEGINNINGS: EGYPTIAN STYLE - 97
RA'S PUSSY FUCKS SHIT UP - 98
SIBLINGS FUCK - 99
DICK IN A BOX - 100
SETH AND HORUS FUCK WITH SALAD - 102
SCORPIONS ARE FUCKING DANGEROUS - 103
SPHINX SURPRISE - 104
DON'T STEAL FROM THE GODS - 106

NORSE MYTHOLOGY

BEGINNINGS: NORSE STYLE - 109
LOKI IS A SHIT STYLIST - 110
THOR LOOKS FUCKING MAGNIFICENT IN A DRESS - 111
LOKI IS A FUCKING SEXY HORSE - 113
THOR AND LOKI GO ON A GIANT ADVENTURE - 114
DON'T FUCK AROUND WITH MISTLETOE - 116
THE VOLSUNGSAGA - 117
SEALS ARE SLIPPERY LITTLE SHITS - 121
ODIN IS SHIT WITH BABIES - 122
DON'T FEED THE GIANT DEMON WOLF MONSTER - 123
BALDUR'S FUCKED UP FUNERAL - 124
LOKI IS A FUCKING AWFUL DRUNK - 125
ODIN IS SHIT AT DATING - 126

MOTHERFUCKING CRAZY MURDER-DWARVES - 127
RETURN OF THE MAGICAL WIZARD MEAD - 128
ELFNAPPING IS A BAD IDEA - 129
THOR THE OVERPROTECTIVE DAD - 130
END OF THE FUCKING NORSE WORLD - 131

AFRICAN MYTHOLOGY

BEGINNINGS: WEST AFRICAN STYLE - 135
POPULATING THE EARTH - 136
BABY SKY GODS - 137
DEATH IS AN ANGRY GIANT - 138
AFRICAN SPIDER-MAN - 140
ANANSI KIDNAPS EVERYONE - 141
ANANSI HAGGLES LIKE A MEAN MOTHERFUCKER - 143
FIRE IS A SHIT FRIEND - 145
TORTOISES ARE SHIT AT CLIMBING TREES - 146

CENTRAL AND SOUTH AMERICAN MYTHOLOGY

BEGINNINGS: AZTEC STYLE - 149
MAKING SUNS IS FUCKING DIFFICULT - 150
WHERE DO PEOPLE COME FROM? - 152
A GODLY PISS-UP - 153
QUETZALCOATL FUCKS UP - 154
TEZCATLIPOCA IS A REALLY SHITTY WISH FAIRY - 155
BEWARE OF THE LLAMA - 156
ANGRY GAY GIANTS - 157
BEGINNINGS: MAYAN STYLE - 158
FOOTBALL WITH DEATH - 159

NATIVE AMERICAN MYTHOLOGY

BEGINNINGS: IROQUOIS STYLE - 163
THE SUN IS A MOTHERFUCKING SEVERED HEAD - 164
ANIMALS ARE VINDICTIVE FUCKS - 165
DEMIGODS KNOW WHAT AMERICA WANTS - 166
MOOWIS THE SEXY SNOWMAN - 167

STEALING A BABY BEAVER - 168
GETTING REVENGE ON THE SUN - 170

BEOWULF

BEOWULF MURDERS A MONSTER - 173
BEOWULF MURDERS A MONSTER'S MUM - 174
BEOWULF GETS HIS JUST DESSERTS - 175

GREEK MYTHOLOGY

THE ILIAD: SHIT THAT HAPPENS BEFORE THE BEGINNING OF THE BOOK

OK SO THE ILIAD IS A GREAT BIG STORY, BUT THERE'S OTHER IMPORTANT SHIT THAT HAPPENS BEFORE THE BEGINNING OF THE MAIN STORY.

HECUBA, THE QUEEN OF TROY, GETS A STRANGE FUCKING DREAM ABOUT GIVING BIRTH TO SOME FUCKING FIRE. THIS MEANS HER NEXT SON WOULD DESTROY TROY, SO WHEN HE'S BORN, DADDY PRIAM DUMPS THE BABY ON A FUCKING MOUNTAIN, BECAUSE HE'S A SHIT DAD.

THE BABY DOESN'T DIE, BECAUSE ALL BABIES LEFT ON GREEK MOUNTAINS ARE FUCKING INDESTRUCTIBLE. IT GROWS UP TO BE PARIS, WHO'S EVEN MORE OF A DICK THAN HIS DAD. ONE DAY PARIS IS WANDERING AROUND ON THE MOUNTAIN WHEN A BUNCH OF GODDESSES APPEAR IN FRONT OF HIM.

THE GODDESSES (HERA, APHRODITE AND ATHENA) ARE HAVING AN ARGUMENT, BECAUSE THAT'S WHAT GODDESSES DO. THEY'RE ALL EVIL AND VINDICTIVE. THEY GIVE HIM AN APPLE AND TELL HIM TO GIVE IT TO THE BEST LOOKING ONE, BECAUSE ASKING A STRAIGHT QUESTION WOULD BE TOO FUCKING EASY.

HERA OFFERS HIM SHITLOADS OF POWER. ATHENA OFFERS HIM WISDOM. APHRODITE OFFERS HIM WOMEN.

PARIS GOES FOR THE WOMEN, BECAUSE HE'S FUCKING STUPID AND THINKS THINGS WILL BE STRAIGHTFORWARD.

THE PROBLEM IS, THE WOMAN IN QUESTION HAPPENS TO ALREADY BE MARRIED. APHRODITE AND PARIS DON'T GIVE A SHIT, THOUGH, AND THEY STEAL HER AND FUCK OFF BACK TO TROY.

UNDERSTANDABLY HER HUSBAND (MENELAUS) IS PRETTY FUCKING ANGRY AT THIS, AND STARTS A WAR.

NICE WORK, PARIS.

THE ILIAD: BOOK I

ONE DAY CHRYSES, A TROJAN PRIEST, SHOWS UP AT THE GREEK CAMP, BECAUSE THE GREEKS HAVE TAKEN HIS DAUGHTER AS A SLAVE. UNDERSTANDABLY HE'S PRETTY FUCKING ANNOYED.

AGAMEMNON, LEADER OF THE GREEKS AND OWNER OF CHRYSES' DAUGHTER, TELLS HIM TO FUCK OFF. HE DOES SO, BUT NOT BEFORE CALLING DOWN A PLAGUE ON THE GREEK CAMP. AND THAT'S WHY YOU DON'T FUCK WITH PRIESTS OF APOLLO. LOTS OF PEOPLE DIE, BUT AGAMEMNON'S SUCH A WANKER THAT HE REFUSES TO HAND OVER THE GIRL BECAUSE THEN HE WOULDN'T HAVE ANY WOMEN. (NO SERIOUSLY HE'S A COMPLETE FUCKING BASTARD, HE SACRIFICED HIS OWN DAUGHTER).

ACHILLES TELLS HIM TO STOP BEING SO FUCKING STUPID BECAUSE PEOPLE ARE DYING AND IT'S GENERALLY BEEN A PRETTY SHIT WEEK FOR EVERYONE. AGAMEMNON TELLS HIM TO FUCK OFF (THIS IS A RECURRING THEME). THEN AGAMEMNON CHANGES HIS MIND AND, BECAUSE HE'S AN ARROGANT BASTARD, HANDS OVER THE GIRL AND TAKES ACHILLES' INSTEAD.

ACHILLES, NOT UNDERSTANDING THAT HE'S A FULL-GROWN MAN AND THAT THIS BEHAVIOUR LOOKS FUCKING RIDICULOUS, TRIES TO KILL HIM AND THEN GOES OFF TO CRY IN HIS TENT LIKE SOME SORT OF ANGRY GINGER MAN-BABY FOR THE REST OF THE WAR.

THE ILIAD: BOOK II

ODYSSEUS BEATS UP A DISABLED MAN. THAT'S ABOUT IT.

APART FROM THE FUCKING CATALOGUE OF SHIPS, WHICH GOES ON FOR PAGES AND PAGES AND IS FUCKING BORING.

THE ILIAD: BOOK III

THE ARMIES MARCH AT EACH OTHER FOR A BIT, AND THEN THEY STOP TO MAKE PLANS.

HECTOR, PARIS' BROTHER AND PRETTY MUCH THE ONLY CHARACTER WITH ANY SENSE, TELLS HIM HE'S A DICK (HE IS) AND THAT LIFE WOULD BE EASIER AND LESS SHITTY IF HE WERE DEAD (IT WOULD BE).

PARIS RESPONDS WITH "NO FUCK OFF I'M TOO SEXY TO MAKE FUN OF". WE TOLD YOU HE WAS A DICK.

THEN HE ARRANGES A DUEL WITH MENELAUS, BECAUSE STEALING HIS WIFE WASN'T ENOUGH AND NOW HE WANTS TO KILL HIM TOO. THEY HAVE A BIT OF A FIGHT. IT'S SHIT. THEY KEEP MISSING. THEN MENELAUS GRABS PARIS BY THE HELMET AND STARTS SWINGING HIM ROUND AND ROUND HIS HEAD, WHICH STARTS STRANGLING PARIS. EVERYTHING WOULD BE A LOT LESS SHIT IF HE SUCCEEDED, BUT OF COURSE HE DOESN'T. THAT WOULD BE TOO FUCKING STRAIGHTFORWARD, AND THAT'S NOT HOW THE GODS WORK.

APHRODITE MAKES PARIS INVISIBLE AND THE TWO OF THEM FUCK OFF BACK TO TROY, LEAVING MENELAUS STANDING THERE WITH AN EMPTY HELMET LIKE THE CONFUSED MOTHERFUCKER HE IS.

THEN APHRODITE DUMPS PARIS IN HIS BEDROOM, WHERE HELEN TELLS HIM SHE WISHES HE WAS DEAD. BUT THEN THEY HAVE SEX SO IT'S NOT ALL BAD.

THE ILIAD: BOOK IV

THERE'S A TRUCE, SO THE GODS (WHO ARE SADISTIC MOTHERFUCKERS THAT LIKE TO WATCH PEOPLE MURDER EACH OTHER) ARE GETTING BORED. ATHENA GOES DOWN TO THE BATTLEFIELD AND BULLIES ONE OF THE TROJANS INTO

BREAKING THE TRUCE BY SHOOTING MENELAUS IN THE LEG, THUS UNINTENTIONALLY INVENTING THE ARROW-TO-THE-KNEE JOKE AND INFLICTING YEARS OF SUFFERING ON THE WORLD.

AGAMEMNON SEES THE BLOOD AND, IN A RARE FIT OF NOT BEING A DICK, TELLS MENELAUS TO GO AND SEE A DOCTOR.

MENELAUS TELLS HIM TO FUCK OFF. THEN HE GOES TO SEE THE DOCTOR ANYWAY.

THEN AGAMEMNON GOES ROUND AND ROUND THE ARMY AND GETS THEM READY TO FIGHT, BECAUSE THE TROJANS BROKE THE TRUCE AND THAT'S JUST NOT FUCKING ACCEPTABLE. HE CALLS ODYSSEUS A COWARD AND ODYSSEUS TELLS HIM TO FUCK OFF. HE CALLS DIOMEDES A COWARD AND DIOMEDES WANTS TO TELL HIM TO FUCK OFF BUT DOESN'T BECAUSE HE HAS SOME FUCKING MANNERS, UNLIKE AGAMEMNON.

AND THEN THEY ALL GO OFF TO KILL PEOPLE.

THE ILIAD: BOOK V

DIOMEDES KILLS EVERYONE. HE RAMPAGES UP AND DOWN THE BATTLEFIELD AND FUCKS UP ALL THE TROJANS' PLANS.

TROJANS ARE STABBED IN THE FACE. TROJANS ARE STABBED IN THE ARM. TROJANS ARE STABBED IN THE NIPPLE. LIMBS ARE HACKED OFF. TONGUES ARE CUT OFF. THERE'S A LOT OF BEHEADING. SPEARS GO THROUGH THROATS AND STOMACHS AND NOSES AND NIPPLES (LOTS OF NIPPLES). BRAINS SPLATTER ALL OVER THE BACKS OF HELMETS. DIOMEDES IS A FUCKING KILLING MACHINE.

AND THEN HE STABS APHRODITE, BECAUSE HE'S FUCKING INSANE AND SHE JUST HAPPENS TO BE THERE.

AND THEN HE STABS ARES. AND ARES RUNS AWAY.

DIOMEDES IS JUST THAT FUCKING AWESOME.

THE ILIAD: BOOK VI

HECTOR GOES HOME TO TROY AND HIS MOTHER OFFERS HIM WINE. HECTOR'S A FUCKING PATHETIC LIGHTWEIGHT SO HE TURNS IT DOWN. THEN HE GOES TO SHOUT AT PARIS AGAIN, BECAUSE PARIS IS A SHITTY HUMAN BEING AND DESERVES IT. ALSO HE'S A FUCKING COWARD AND DIDN'T GO OUT TO FIGHT.

HELEN MOANS ABOUT HOW SHE'S A FUCKING TERRIBLE PERSON (SHE IS), AND THEN HECTOR LEAVES BECAUSE HE CAN'T TAKE ANY MORE OF THIS BULLSHIT.

THEN HE GOES TO SEE HIS WIFE, WHO TELLS HIM TO STOP BEING SO FUCKING STUPID AND TO JUST COME HOME FOR A BIT. HE SAYS NO BECAUSE HE NEEDS TO GO AND KILL THINGS WITH A SWORD, THEN HE TRIES TO PICK UP HIS BABY SON, WHO PANICS BECAUSE HECTOR'S WEARING A FUCKING MASSIVE SHINY HELMET AND IT'S FUCKING TERRIFYING.

HECTOR AND ANDROMACHE JUST LAUGH AT HIM. EVEN THE NICE CHARACTERS ARE SHIT PARENTS.

THEN HE GOES OUT TO KILL STUFF AGAIN.

THE ILIAD: BOOK VII

HECTOR RUNS UP TO THE GREEK LINES AND ASKS FOR A DUEL. ALL THE GREEKS LOOK A BIT AWKWARD AND REFUSE TO VOLUNTEER BECAUSE THEY'RE SCARED OF HIM, WHICH IS

UNDERSTANDABLE. HECTOR IS ONE DANGEROUS MOTHERFUCKER.

IN THE END AJAX GETS VOLUNTEERED. AJAX IS BASICALLY THE BRIAN BLESSED OF THE GREEK WORLD. HE'S FUCKING MASSIVE AND SHOUTY.

THEY HIT EACH OTHER WITH ROCKS FOR A BIT UNTIL SOMEONE COMES OVER AND TELLS THEM TO FUCK OFF AND STOP BEING STUPID BECAUSE EVERYONE ELSE HAS HAD ENOUGH AND JUST WANTS TO FUCK OFF BACK HOME. EVENTUALLY THEY STOP, SWAP CLOTHES, AND GO HOME.

THE ILIAD: BOOK VIII

PEOPLE KILL EACH OTHER.

THAT'S IT.

THAT IS GENUINELY EVERYTHING THAT HAPPENS IN BOOK VIII.

NO FUCK OFF WE'RE NOT GOING TO DESCRIBE IT IN DETAIL, IT GOES ON FOR AGES AND NOTHING INTERESTING HAPPENS. UNLESS YOU'RE INTERESTED IN MANGLINGS, THAT IS (AND WHO ISN'T?).

THE ILIAD: BOOK IX

AGAMEMNON REALISES HE'S BEEN A MASSIVE DICK AND SHOULD PROBABLY SAY SORRY TO ACHILLES, WHO'S STILL CRYING IN HIS TENT BECAUSE HE'S SO FUCKING EMOTIONAL.

AGAMEMNON DOESN'T UNDERSTAND FUCKING APOLOGIES THOUGH, SO INSTEAD OF JUST SAYING SORRY HE OFFERS ACHILLES SHITLOADS OF GOLD AND WOMEN AND HORSES. HE

SENDS ODYSSEUS AND AJAX AND PHOENIX TO DO IT THOUGH BECAUSE HE'S STILL A PRETTY SHITTY PERSON AND HE THINKS ACHILLES IS LESS LIKELY TO TELL THEM TO FUCK OFF.

THEY GO TO ACHILLES' TENT AND HAVE A PARTY AND TELL SOME STORIES THAT GO ON FOR FUCKING AGES, AND THEN ACHILLES TELLS THEM ALL TO FUCK OFF. AGAIN.

THE ILIAD: BOOK X

NONE OF THE GREEKS CAN SLEEP, BECAUSE THEY'RE ALL TOO FUCKING SCARED OF BEING MURDERED IN THEIR BEDS BY ALL THE ANGRY TROJANS. ODYSSEUS AND DIOMEDES SNEAK OUT OF BED IN THE MIDDLE OF THE NIGHT AND GO OUT TO FUCK SHIT UP.

THEY KILL A FEW TROJANS AND THEN THEY STEAL AS MANY HORSES AS THEY CAN CARRY, WHICH IS ONE HELL OF A LOT OF FUCKING HORSES. AND THEN THEY GO BACK TO BED

THE ILIAD: BOOK XI

THERE'S YET ANOTHER FUCKING BATTLE. AGAMEMNON KILLS FUCKLOADS OF TROJANS AND STEALS THEIR CLOTHES. AND THEN HE GETS WOUNDED, WHICH IS HIS OWN FUCKING FAULT FOR STEALING CLOTHES INSTEAD OF DEFENDING HIMSELF.

WITH AGAMEMNON OUT OF THE WAY, THE GREEKS START LOSING. PARIS SHOOTS DIOMEDES IN THE FOOT AND THEN RUNS UP TO TAKE THE PISS OUT OF HIM. DIOMEDES TELLS HIM TO FUCK OFF AND LAUGHS AT HOW GIRLY HIS HAIR IS.

IT'S FUCKING CHAOS. ALL THE GREEKS ARE BEING WOUNDED OR DYING, AND THEN SOMEONE SUGGESTS THAT PATROCLUS MIGHT WANT TO TELL ACHILLES TO MAN UP AND STOP SULKING. AS WE ALL KNOW THIS IS A FUCKING STUPID IDEA AND IT'S NOT GOING TO END WELL.

THE ILIAD: BOOK XII

THE GREEKS HAVE BUILT A WALL. IT'S A FUCKING HUGE WALL. IT'S COMPLETELY FUCKING UNBREAKABLE. KIND OF LIKE HELM'S DEEP BUT GREEK. THERE IS NO WAY TO BREAK IT.

THAT'S RIGHT, HECTOR BREAKS IT. WITH A ROCK. HE REALLY IS ONE DESTRUCTIVE MOTHERFUCKER.

THE ILIAD: BOOK XIII

PEOPLE DIE. MORE PEOPLE DIE.

YES, THAT'S RIGHT, IT'S ANOTHER FUCKING BATTLE CHAPTER.

THE ILIAD: BOOK XIV

HERA TRICKS ZEUS INTO LETTING HER PLAY WITH THE BATTLE.

THAT'S RIGHT, YET ANOTHER FUCKING BATTLE CHAPTER. THIS TIME, HOWEVER, HERA'S SHITTY INFLUENCE MEANS THE GREEKS WIN.

OH, AND SOMEBODY'S EYEBALL FALLS OUT. THAT'S ABOUT IT.

THE ILIAD: BOOK XV

ZEUS WAKES UP, SEES HECTOR BLEEDING ON THE FLOOR AND SHOUTS AT HERA FOR BEING EVIL. SHE IS. SHE'S FUCKING EVIL.

AND THEN THE GODS HAVE A FUCKING MASSIVE ARGUMENT. AGAIN. THE RESULT OF THIS IS THAT APOLLO COMES DOWN TO THE BATTLEFIELD AND TELLS HECTOR TO MAN THE FUCK UP AND GO AND KILL SOME GREEKS.

HECTOR MANS THE FUCK UP AND GOES AND KILLS SOME GREEKS. A LOT OF GREEKS. HE'S ON FUCKING FIRE. LITERALLY.

THE ILIAD: BOOK XVI

PATROCLUS HAS JUST SEEN SOME PEOPLE GET A BIT MANGLED AND SO IS PRETTY FUCKING UPSET. HE'S IN TEARS. HE GOES TO VISIT ACHILLES, WHO LAUGHS AT HIM, CALLS HIM A GIRL AND MAKES FUN OF HIS DISTRESS (ACHILLES IS A SHIT FRIEND).

PATROCLUS TELLS ACHILLES THAT EVERYONE'S DEAD AND IT'S BECAUSE ACHILLES IS BEING FUCKING STUPID AND SULKING, AND ACHILLES (WHO IS EGOTISTICAL AND A BIT OF A DICK) INTERPRETS THIS TO BE A COMMENT ABOUT HOW WONDERFUL HE IS INSTEAD. IN THE END, THOUGH, HE AGREES TO LET PATROCLUS PUT ON HIS ARMOUR AND PRETEND TO BE HIM.

WHAT A FUCKING TERRIBLE IDEA.

HE PUTS ON ACHILLES' CLOTHES, BUT HE LEAVES THE SPEAR BEHIND. ACHILLES'S SPEAR IS SO FUCKING MASSIVE THAT NOBODY ELSE CAN PICK IT UP. THEN HE TAKES THE MYRMIDONS AND GOES OUT TO FUCK SHIT UP FOR THE TROJANS.

THEN THERE'S YET ANOTHER FUCKING BATTLE SCENE. LOTS OF STABBING, A COUPLE OF BEHEADINGS, A GUY GETS HIS HEAD SPLIT IN HALF WITH A ROCK, SOMEONE TAKES A SPEAR TO THE

MOUTH WHICH SMASHES IN ALL HIS TEETH THEN COMES OUT THE BACK OF HIS HEAD. THE USUAL STUFF. THE TROJANS START RUNNING AWAY.

PATROCLUS CHASES THEM AND KILLS SARPEDON. ZEUS IS A BIT UPSET, BECAUSE SARPEDON WAS FUCKING AWESOME, SO HE MAKES IT RAIN BLOOD FOR A BIT. THERE'S A FIGHT OVER THE BODY IN THE DARK AND THE BLOOD RAIN. IT'S ALL INCREDIBLY FUCKING OVERDRAMATIC.

PATROCLUS KILLS EVERYONE, BUT THEN APOLLO SMACKS HIM OVER THE HEAD AND STEALS HIS CLOTHES, LEAVING HIM FAR TOO FUCKING VULNERABLE AND GENERALLY IN A BIT OF A SHIT SITUATION.

AND THEN HE DIES.

HECTOR STABS HIM A BIT, THEN HE TELLS HECTOR TO ENJOY LIFE WHILE IT LASTS, THEN HECTOR STABS HIM A BIT MORE. AND A BIT MORE. AND SOME MORE. AND THEN HIS SPEAR BREAKS, BUT HE KEEPS GOING.

AND NOW PATROCLUS IS FUCKING DEAD. IT'S ONE OF THE SADDEST SCENES IN THE ENTIRE FUCKING POEM.

THE ILIAD: BOOK XVII

MENELAUS NOTICES THAT PATROCLUS IS DEAD. HE'S FUCKING FURIOUS. HE RUNS OVER TO THE BODY AND KILLS FUCKLOADS OF TROJANS THAT ARE TRYING TO STRIP IT.

HE'S NOT FAST ENOUGH, THOUGH, AND HECTOR FUCKS OFF WITH ACHILLES' ARMOUR AND PUTS IT ON, JUST TO RUB IT IN A BIT.

THEN THERE'S YET ANOTHER FUCKING BATTLE SCENE, EXCEPT THIS TIME IT'S ALL TAKING PLACE AROUND PATROCLUS' DEAD

BODY, WHICH HAPPENS TO BE COMPLETELY STARK FUCKING NAKED.

THE ILIAD: BOOK XVIII

ANTILOCHUS TELLS ACHILLES THAT PATROCLUS IS DEAD. AND NAKED. AND LEFT OUT ON THE FLOOR.

ACHILLES HAS A MASSIVE FUCKING BREAKDOWN, SOBS, TEARS HIS HAIR OUT AND LIES ON THE FLOOR REFUSING TO GET UP. ALL THE SERVANTS HOLD HIS HANDS BECAUSE THEY THINK HE MIGHT CUT HIS OWN THROAT. IT'S PRETTY FUCKING UNDIGNIFIED.

HIS MUM HEARS HIM CRYING AND COMES TO TRY TO HELP. HE TELLS HER HE WISHES SHE'D NEVER HAD HIM, AND SHE STARTS CRYING TOO. ACHILLES IS A SHIT SON AS WELL AS A SHIT FRIEND. ACHILLES IS GENERALLY A BIT OF A WANKER.

THEN AFTER HE'S CALMED DOWN HE STANDS ON THE WALLS AND SHOUTS FOR A BIT, AND EVERYONE FEELS A BIT BETTER. ACHILLES SHOUTS REALLY FUCKING LOUDLY.

THETIS FUCKS OFF, LEAVING ACHILLES STANDING AROUND SHOUTING, AND GETS HEPHAESTUS TO MAKE HIM SOME NEW ARMOUR (HECTOR STOLE HIS OLD ARMOUR OFF PATROCLUS' DEAD BODY). ALL THE ARMOUR IS FUCKING MAGNIFICENT, AND THE SHIELD IS MAGIC AND HAS MOVING PICTURES OF EVERYTHING ON IT.

NO REALLY. EVERYTHING. EVERYTHING IN THE ENTIRE FUCKING WORLD.

THE ILIAD: BOOK XIX

ACHILLES AND AGAMEMNON SAY SORRY TO EACH OTHER. THAT'S ALL THAT HAPPENS.

OH, AND THEN ACHILLES PUTS ON HIS ARMOUR AND GETS READY TO KILL AS MANY TROJANS AS HE POSSIBLY CAN. ACHILLES IS FUCKING FURIOUS.

THE ILIAD: BOOK XX

THE GODS JOIN IN WITH THE BATTLE THIS TIME.

YES THAT'S RIGHT, ANOTHER FUCKING BATTLE. THIS TIME IT'S ACHILLES KILLING EVERYONE. QUITE A LOT OF THEM HE JUST RUNS OVER WITH HIS CHARIOT, WHICH IS VERY MESSY AND KIND OF DICKISH AND UNCHIVALROUS.

THE ILIAD: BOOK XXI

ACHILLES ATTACKS A FUCKING RIVER.

NO, SERIOUSLY. *HE FIGHTS A MOTHERFUCKING RIVER.*

THE ILIAD: BOOK XXII

ACHILLES SHOUTS AT APOLLO FOR A BIT. THAT'S RIGHT, HE SHOUTS AT A FUCKING GOD. THEN HE SPOTS HECTOR STANDING AROUND OUTSIDE TROY AND RUNS AT HIM.

HECTOR'S JUST STANDING THERE, LOOKING LOST, AS ACHILLES SPRINTS ACROSS THE BATTLEFIELD TOWARDS HIM. PRIAM WEEPS AND TEARS OUT HIS HAIR. HECTOR JUST STANDS THERE. HE'S MAKING HIS OWN FUCKING FATHER CRY, AND HE JUST DOESN'T DO ANYTHING. HECUBA TAKES HER TOP OFF AND CRIES, AND HECTOR JUST STANDS THERE. HIS PARENTS ARE SO FUCKING UNDIGNIFIED, AND HE DOESN'T GIVE A SHIT.

THEN HECTOR HAS A BIT OF INTERNAL CONFLICT AND TRIES TO DECIDE WHETHER TO RUN AWAY OR NOT, BUT NO. NO FUCKING WAY IS HE GOING TO RUN AWAY. HE JUST STANDS THERE. THEN ACHILLES REACHES HIM, AND HE RUNS AWAY.

THEY RUN ROUND AND ROUND TROY FOR FUCKING AGES, BEFORE THE GODS DECIDE TO INTERVENE BECAUSE THIS IS JUST FUCKING RIDICULOUS. ATHENA PRETENDS TO BE HECTOR'S BROTHER, PROMISES TO HELP HIM, AND THEN FUCKS OFF BACK TO OLYMPUS, HAVING DISTRACTED HIM ENOUGH FOR ACHILLES TO CATCH UP.

HECTOR TELLS ACHILLES THAT THEY SHOULD MAKE A DEAL AND TREAT WHOEVER DIES PROPERLY. ACHILLES TELLS HIM TO FUCK OFF (WHAT A FUCKING SURPRISE).

ACHILLES THROWS HIS SPEAR AND MISSES. HECTOR DOES THE SAME. THEN HE TURNS ROUND TO GET HELP FROM HIS FRIEND, BUT THE FRIEND HAS GONE. HE WAS ACTUALL ATHENA IN DISGUISE. SURPRISE, BITCH. THEN ATHENA PICKS UP ACHILLES' SPEAR AND GIVES IT BACK, WHICH IS JUST FUCKING UNFAIR. HECTOR PULLS OUT HIS SWORD, AND ACHILLES STABS HIM THROUGH THE NECK WITH HIS SPEAR.

HECTOR BEGS ACHILLES TO GIVE HIS BODY TO PRIAM AND HECUBA, BUT ACHILLES TELLS HIM TO FUCK OFF. AGAIN. THEN HE WAITS A COUPLE OF MINUTES FOR HECTOR TO DIE BEFORE STRIPPING THE BODY NAKED, STICKING LEATHER CORDS THROUGH THE ANKLES, TYING IT TO THE BACK OF HIS CHARIOT AND THEN DRIVING ROUND AND ROUND TROY, WAVING THE BODY AT HECTOR'S PARENTS. IN CASE YOU HADN'T NOTICED YET, ACHILLES IS A DICK.

PRIAM AND HECUBA CRY ONE HELL OF A LOT, AND THEN SOMEBODY GOES TO TELL ANDROMACHE THAT HER HUSBAND'S DEAD, BECAUSE SHE FORGOT TO GO AND WATCH THE FUCKING BATTLE. SHE FAINTS. THEN SHE WAKES UP AND CRIES. THEN THE BABY CRIES. EVERYONE IS FUCKING CRYING, AND ACHILLES IS STILL DRAGGING HECTOR ROUND AND ROUND THE CITY. WHAT A DICK.

THE ILIAD: BOOK XXIII

ACHILLES AND ALL THE OTHER GREEKS GO HOME, AND THEN ACHILLES REMEMBERS THAT PATROCLUS IS DEAD.

SHIT.

HE SAYS "OH SHIT PATROCLUS IS DEAD", AND ALL THE GREEKS START CRYING.

THEN THEY HAVE A FUCKING MASSIVE PARTY, AND WHILE ACHILLES IS PASSED OUT ON THE FLOOR TRYING NOT TO BE TOO FUCKING MISERABLE, THE GHOST OF PATROCLUS COMES TO VISIT HIM. PATROCLUS TELLS HIM SOME SHIT ABOUT HOW SAD HIS LIFE WAS, AND ACHILLES TRIES TO HUG HIM. PATROCLUS IS A FUCKING GHOST THOUGH, SO ACHILLES' ARMS GO RIGHT THROUGH HIM. PATROCLUS VANISHES, AND ACHILLES STARTS CRYING AGAIN.

ALL THE GREEKS MAKE A FUCKING MASSIVE MOUNTAIN OF WOOD, SHOVE PATROCLUS' BODY ON TOP, AND SET FIRE TO IT

ALL. THEN ACHILLES THROWS SOME SHEEP AND SOME HONEY AND SOME HORSES AND SOME TROJANS AND SOME DOGS ON THE FIRE. THAT'S JUST HOW FUCKING UPSET HE IS. HE'S LITERALLY SETTING FIRE TO PUPPIES.

THEN THEY HAVE SHITLOADS OF FUNERAL GAMES, AND EVERYONE CHEATS, BECAUSE ALL GREEKS ARE FUCKING AWFUL PEOPLE.

THE ILIAD: BOOK XXIV

THIS IS IT, MOTHERFUCKERS. THIS IS THE END OF THE ENTIRE FUCKING ILIAD.

ACHILLES CAN'T SLEEP, SO HE HOPS IN HIS CHARIOT AND DRAGS HECTOR ROUND AND ROUND PATROCLUS' TOMB, BECAUSE BEING A DICK MAKES HIM FEEL BETTER.

ZEUS SENDS IRIS DOWN FROM OLYMPUS TO HAVE A CHAT WITH PRIAM, WHO IS SITTING ON THE FLOOR CRYING, SURROUNDED BY HIS KIDS, WHO ARE ALSO ALL CRYING. PRIAM HAS FIFTY SONS, SO THAT'S ONE HELL OF A LOT OF CRYING. THEY HAVE A CHAT, AND PRIAM SETS OFF TO RESCUE HECTOR'S BODY. GIVEN THAT PRIAM IS FUCKING ANCIENT, IT'S A PRETTY SHIT PLAN. HE TELLS HECUBA AND SHE TELLS HIM NOT TO EVEN THINK ABOUT FUCKING OFF TO THE GREEK CAMP AND ALSO THAT SHE WANTS TO RIP ACHILLES' LIVER OUT WITH HER TEETH.

SHE'S KIND OF SCARY, BUT PRIAM DOESN'T LISTEN. HE FUCKS OFF TO THE GREEK CAMP WITH A FUCKING MASSIVE PILE OF TREASURE. ZEUS SEES A TINY LITTLE OLD MAN IN TEARS WALKING ACROSS THE PLAIN, AND SENDS HERMES DOWN TO HELP HIM.

THE TWO OF THEM GO TO THE GREEK CAMP, AND THEN HERMES FUCKS OFF, LEAVING PRIAM TO HANDLE ACHILLES ON HIS OWN. ALL GODS ARE DICKS.

PRIAM TELLS DAD STORIES TO ACHILLES FOR A BIT AND MAKES HIM CRY. THEN THAT MAKES PRIAM START CRYING AGAIN. THEY SIT ON THE FLOOR SOBBING FOR FUCKING AGES (IT'S REALLY FUCKING TRAGIC), THEN ACHILLES AGREES TO GIVE THE BODY BACK AND SAYS HE'S SORRY FOR ALL THE AWFUL SHIT HE DID TO IT.

THEN THEY HAVE A PARTY.

LATER, PRIAM TAKES THE BODY BACK TO TROY. EVERYONE CRIES. IT'S FUCKING MISERABLE. THEN THEY BURN AND BURY THE BODY. EVERYONE'S STILL CRYING.

THAT'S THE END. FUCKING UPSETTING, ISN'T IT?

LET'S TALK ABOUT HERACLES

YES. THAT'S FUCKING HERACLES. NOT HERCULES. WE'RE TALKING GREEK MYTHS HERE.

FIRSTLY - EVERYTHING DISNEY TOLD YOU AS A CHILD IS FUCKING LIES. THE DISNEY HERCULES MOVIE TRAMPLES ON THE MYTHS, THEN URINATES ON THEM, THEN FUCKING DRAGS THEM AROUND THE WALLS OF TROY.

STILL A GREAT MOVIE THOUGH.

ANYWAY. HERACLES.

THIS GUY AMPHITRYON IS MARRIED TO ALCMENE. SHE'S FUCKING WHINY AND WON'T SLEEP WITH HIM UNTIL HE GOES AND AVENGES HER BROTHERS (YEAH, THEY'RE DEAD, BUT IT'S NOT FUCKING IMPORTANT).

SO HE FUCKS OFF TO BE AN AVENGER, LEAVING HIS YOUNG, HOT WIFE ALL ALONE IN BED. SO GUESS WHO FUCKING JUMPS ON THIS OPPORTUNITY TO TAP THAT?

THAT'S RIGHT - ZEUS. HE IMPERSONATES HER HUSBAND AND SLEEPS WITH HER. ALL NIGHT. EXCEPT BECAUSE HE'S ZEUS HE MADE THE NIGHT LAST FOR THREE FUCKING DAYS - THAT'S STAMINA RIGHT THERE. AND BECAUSE IT'S ZEUS OF COURSE THERE ARE GOING TO BE MAGIC BABIES.

NINE MONTHS DOWN THE LINE ZEUS LETS SLIP THAT HE'S ABOUT TO HAVE ANOTHER SON, SO HERA IS NATURALLY PRETTY FUCKING PISSED OFF ABOUT THIS (AS USUAL). SHE TRICKS HIM INTO MAKING SOME DIVINE PROMISE BULLSHIT THAT THE FIRST CHILD BORN THAT NIGHT WOULD BECOME HIGH KING.

GREAT, HERACLES GETS TO BE HIGH KING! OR NOT. HERA DOES SOME MORE WEIRD-ASS MAGIC TO DELAY THE BIRTH OF HERACLES BY A FEW HOURS, AND MAKE HIS COUSIN

EURYSTHEUS BE BORN PREMATURELY - SO THE DIVINE PROMISE BULLSHIT GOES TO HIM.

SO HERACLES GETS A RIVAL AND A GODDESS WHO HATES HIM RIGHT FROM BIRTH. HOW FUCKING LUCKY. HERA IS SO PISSED OFF AT CUTE BABY HERACLES THAT SHE SENDS TWO MURDEROUS SNAKES WITH FUCKING LASER EYES AND SHIT TO COME AND EAT HIM, BUT BECAUSE HE'S FUCKING HERACLES HE STRANGLES THEM BECAUSE THAT SHOULD BE EVERY NEWBORN BABY'S REACTION TO REPTILES.

HERACLES FUCKS SHIT UP

ICKLE BABY HERACLES GROWS UP BIG AND STRONG. NO FUCKING SURPRISES THERE. THEN HE GETS FAMOUS THROUGH THE ONLY WAY TO BE A CELEBRITY IN MYTHOLOGY - GRATUITOUSLY SLAUGHTERING SHITLOADS OF PEOPLE.

HE DEFEATS SO MANY ENEMIES THAT HE GETS AWARDED A HOT ASS PRINCESS - MEGARA. THEY HAVE SOME KIDS TOGETHER AND EVERYTHING IS FUCKING GREAT. HERACLES CONTINUES TO EXCESSIVELY SLAUGHTER (ONE TIME HE HAS SOMEONE RIPPED IN TWO BY HORSES. NOW THAT'S JUST MESSY). THIS KIND OF PISSES OFF HERA. PRETTY MUCH EVERYTHING PISSES OFF HERA.

SHE MAKES HIM MAD. LIKE SERIOUSLY FUCKING MAD. HE KILLS HIS WIFE AND KIDS WITHOUT REALISING IT, THEN REMEMBERS AND CRIES FUCKING MANLY TEARS FOR A BIT. WHEN HE GETS HIS SHIT TOGETHER, HE GOES TO DELPHI TO THE PYTHIA FOR FUCKING COUNSELLING (THE PYTHIA IS A CRAZY OLD LADY WHO SPEAKS THE PROPHECY OF APOLLO). SHE TELLS HIM HE HAS TO GO AND DO WHATEVER EURYSTHEUS TELLS HIM TO DO FOR 12 FUCKING YEARS. THEN THAT WOULD MAKE UP FOR SLAUGHTERING HIS OWN FAMILY AND ALSO GIVE HIM IMMORTALITY. SWEET.

THERE'S ANOTHER VERSION WHERE HE DID ALL HIS TASKS FOR EURYSTHEUS BECAUSE THEY WERE A COUPLE. HOWEVER, WE DON'T SHIP IT, SO LET'S JUST GO WITH THE WHOLE DOING-THE-TASKS-TO-GET-IMMORTALITY BUSINESS.

THE LABOURS OF HERACLES: I - THE NEMEAN LION

WHEN HERACLES GETS TO EURYSTHEUS' PALACE IN TIRYNS, EURYSTHEUS CLEARLY HASN'T RECENTLY WATCHED THE LION KING AND DECIDES TO TELL HERACLES TO GO KILL A FUCKING ADORABLE LION.

OH BUT IT'S NOT JUST YOUR REGULAR SIMBA. OH NO, THIS IS A FUCKING IRON PROOF, BRONZE PROOF, WHATEVER PROOF MAGIC MURDER LION. IT'S ONE INDESTRUCTIBLE MOTHERFUCKER. IT ALSO LIKES EATING PEOPLE, AND LIVES IN A SNUG LITTLE CAVE NEAR NEMEA; HENCE NEMEAN LION.

OF COURSE HERACLES HITS THE LION WITH THE RIDICULOUS NUMBER OF WEAPONS HE CARRIES AROUND (WHY DOES HE NEED A FUCKING CLUB *AND* A SWORD?). THIS IS FUCKING STUPID BECAUSE THE LION'S MERELY MILDLY AMUSED BY THIS. THEN HERACLES JUST FUCKING STRANGLES IT BECAUSE THAT'S HOW TO SOLVE ANY PROBLEM.

HERACLES TAKES THE STINKY DEAD LION BACK TO EURYSTHEUS, WHO IS SO FUCKING TERRIFIED HE HAS SOMEONE MAKE HIM A MASSIVE FUCKING JAR TO HIDE IN. WHAT A LOSER.

HERACLES THEN REALISES FUR IS REALLY FUCKING IN THIS SEASON, SKINS THE LION AND MAKES A FLASHY EVERYTHING-PROOF CLOAK OUT OF IT.

THE LABOURS OF HERACLES: II - THE LERNAEAN HYDRA

HAIL HYDRA, BITCHES.

FOR CHALLENGE NUMBER TWO, HERACLES HAS TO KILL ANOTHER FUCKING MONSTER. THIS TIME IT'S A FUCKING HUGE DOG, WITH A SHIT-TONNE (EIGHT OR NINE OR FUCKING FIFTY) OF SNAKEY HEADS. THIS IS ONE BAD ASS MOTHERFUCKER, BECAUSE GUESS WHAT? IT HAS FUCKING POISON BREATH. YOU DON'T WANT TO SMOOCH THIS BITCH.

HERACLES RUNS INTO THE HYDRA'S COSY SWAMP HOME AND STARTS BEATING IT UP. WHAT A FUCKING JERK. HE SQUISHES ALL THE HEADS, BUT IT DOESN'T FUCKING DIE, IT GROWS MORE HEADS. LIKE A WORM. BUT NOT LIKE A WORM. DON'T FUCKING BEAT UP WORMS. UNLESS THEY HAVE LOTS OF POISONOUS HEADS AND ATTACK YOU FIRST.

ANYWAY, ATHENA EVENTUALLY TELLS HIM THAT HE SHOULD BURN THOSE HEADS SO THEY DON'T COME BACK (ATHENA TOTALLY HAS THE HOTS FOR HERACLES). SO HERACLES BURNS THOSE BITCHES AND THE HYDRA DIES. PRO TIP: BURN YOUR PROBLEMS.

OH BUT EURYSTHEUS ISN'T FUCKING HAPPY (EURYSTHEUS IS NEVER HAPPY; HE'S A WHINY LITTLE SHIT) BECAUSE HERACLES CHEATED (HIS BEST BUDDY IOLAUS BROUGHT HIM THE FLAME-THROWERS). BITCH.

THE LABOURS OF HERACLES: III - THE CERYNEIAN HIND

THE FIRST LABOUR THAT DOESN'T HAVE SENSELESS MURDER, SORRY. (SORRY SHOULD ALWAYS BE INTERPRETED AS "FUCK YOU" IN THIS BOOK).

HERACLES HAS TO GO CATCH A GENDER-CONFUSED DEER CREATURE (AND NOT FUCKING KILL IT). THIS DEER IS FUCKING SHINY THOUGH, AND SACRED TO ARTEMIS. HERACLES HAS TO CATCH BAMBI'S MUM, BUT IN A SUPER-SAFETY CONSCIOUS WAY. NOT HIS FUCKING STYLE.

HE TAKES A WHOLE FUCKING YEAR TO CATCH THE DEER AND SOMEHOW MANAGES TO FUCKING SHOOT ITS LEGS TOGETHER WITH AN ARROW WITHOUT HURTING IT. HE MUST HAVE A FUCKING VETERINARY DEGREE. BUT ARTEMIS STILL GETS PISSED OFF WITH HER THUGGISH HALF BROTHER, SO HE PASSES THE BLAME OFF TO EURYSTHEUS. WHAT A GUY.

OH AND THERE'S A THEORY THAT THE DEER ISS A FUCKING REINDEER. GO, CHILDREN, AND KIDNAP RUDOLPH. BUT IN A NON-MURDEROUS WAY. THIS IS PROBABLY THE ONLY TIME WE'LL EVER TELL YOU *NOT* TO MURDER ANYTHING.

THE LABOURS OF HERACLES: IV - THE ERYMANTHIAN BOAR

BECAUSE HERACLES IS SO FUCKING GREAT AT ANIMAL HERDING, THE NEXT TASK IS TO ROUND UP A MASSIVE FUCKING BOAR.
ON THE WAY TO HIS NEXT BIT OF SENSELESS ANIMAL CRUELTY, HERACLES RUNS INTO SOME CENTAUR BROS AND GETS COMPLETELY FUCKING SHIT-FACED (CENTAURS ALWAYS GET YOU DRUNK. FACT.) AS USUAL WITH HERACLES, THINGS SOON GO TO SHIT. VIOLENT SHIT. HE ACCIDENTALLY KILLS HIS LIAM NEESON-ESQUE MENTOR FIGURE, CHIRON. GOOD GOING HERACLES. THEN SOME OTHER CENTAUR GETS CURIOUS ABOUT HERACLES' REALLY FUCKING NASTY LOOKING ARROWS. AND KILLS HIMSELF WITH THEM. THIS IS WHY HERACLES HAS NO FRIENDS.

WHEN HE FUCKING FINALLY SOBERS UP, HERACLES GOES PIG HUNTING. HOW TO CATCH A FUCKING BADASS BOAR: SHOUT AT IT UNTIL IT GETS SCARED, THROW IT IN SOME FUCKING SNOW, THEN SIT ON IT. BECAUSE YOU'RE HERACLES, AND YOU CAN DO SHIT LIKE THAT.

HE THEN JUST AWKWARDLY DUMPS IT IN MYCENAE, BECAUSE HE HAS OTHER PARTIES TO ATTEND (SOME ADVENTURE WITH THIS JASON ASSHOLE, NO FUCKING BIGGIE).

THE LABOURS OF HERACLES: V - THE STABLES OF AUGEIAS

HERACLES GETS A PART TIME JOB AS A STABLE HAND. EXCEPT IT'S ONLY FOR ONE FUCKING DAY, HE'S NOT PAID AND EURYSTHEUS JUST REALLY LIKES THE IDEA OF HERACLES SHOVELLING SHIT. LIKE A SHIT-TONNE OF FUCKING SHIT.

AUGEIAS IS THIS LAZY SHIT WHO LITERALLY NEVER FUCKING CLEANS UP AFTER HIS TONNES OF BARNYARD ANIMALS. HERACLES HAS TO CLEAN UP HIS SHIT IN JUST ONE DAY. THIS IS A PROBLEM BECAUSE THESE COWS ARE FUCKING ANGRY AND JUST FUCKING ATTACK HIM FOR NO REASON.

INSTEAD OF ACTUALLY TOUCHING THE STINKY SHIT HIMSELF, HERACLES DIVERTS SOME FRIENDLY NEIGHBOURHOOD RIVERS TO CLEAN UP THIS SHIT. HE HAS NO FUCKING CONCERN FOR AQUATIC ENVIRONMENTS. WHAT A SHITBAG.

EURYSTHEUS SAYS THAT THIS ONE DOESN'T EVEN FUCKING COUNT BECAUSE HERACLES DIDN'T ACTUALLY DO ANYTHING HIMSELF. WHAT A BITCH. MESSAGE OF THE DAY: CLEAN UP AFTER YOUR FUCKING PETS.

THE LABOURS OF HERACLES: VI - THE STYMPHALIAN BIRDS

THIS TIME HERACLES HAS TO GET RID OF ANOTHER FUCKING MYTHICAL DEADLY PEST PROBLEM. THE STYMPHALIAN BIRDS ARE MAGIC BRONZE DUCKS WITH FUCKING RAZOR FEATHERS. OH AND THEY SHIT POISON. DO NOT PUT THEM IN YOUR FUCKING BATHTUB.

HERACLES WADES INTO THEIR MARSH LIKE THE BIG FUCKING OAF HE IS, AND HE'S SURPRISED TO FIND THAT SHOOTING THEM WITH ARROWS IS COMPLETELY FUCKING USELESS.

THEN ATHENA GIVES HERACLES SOME REALLY FUCKING ANNOYING CASTANETS TO PLAY, AND HE'S SO FUCKING BAD AT THEM AND MAKES SUCH A FUCKING NOISE THAT THE RAZOR-DEATH-DUCKIES FLY AWAY. THEN THEY JUST PLAGUE OTHER PEOPLE, CAUSING UNTOLD FUCKING DEATH AND DESTRUCTION. GOOD FUCKING WORK HERACLES.

THE LABOURS OF HERACLES: VII - THE CRETAN BULL

CRETE HAS A FUCK-TONNE OF COWS. AND HERACLES ONLY HAS TO GET THE FUCKING FIRE-BREATHING ONE. WHICH IS ALSO THE VERY SAME ONE THAT THE QUEEN OF CRETE HAD FALLEN IN LOVE WITH. EW.

HERACLES ALMOST GETS FLAME-GRILLED BY THIS BULL, BUT EVENTUALLY CATCHES IT AND BRINGS IT BACK TO EURYSTHEUS. GOOD JOB HERACLES (THIS IS POSSIBLY THE ONLY TIME WE'LL SAY THAT NON-SARCASTICALLY). BUT THEN EURYSTHEUS JUST LETS IT FUCKING GO AND IT WANDERS AROUND GREECE FOR A WHILE, TRYING TO CAMEO IN AS MANY FUCKING MYTHS AS POSSIBLE. WHAT A FUCKING DIVA.

THE LABOURS OF HERACLES: VIII - THE MARES OF DIOMEDES

NO, NOT THE SAME DIOMEDES FROM THE ILIAD. THIS GUY IS MORE OF AN ASSHOLE. I MEAN, HE FUCKING FEEDS HIS GUESTS TO HIS EVIL HORSES. THAT'S NOT FUCKING XENIA, MATE.

OF COURSE HERACLES HAS TO STEAL THESE CRAZY-ASS HORSES, AND MANAGES TO TAKE SOME 'VOLUNTEERS' WITH HIM TO HELP. YES, ALL HIS FRIENDS ARE PROBABLY FUCKING EATEN - ARE YOU REALLY SURPRISED? HE THEN SOMEHOW CAUSES A MINOR FLOOD (THIS GUY REALLY SHOULD FUCKING STOP MESSING WITH RIVERS, THEY HAVE FEELINGS TOO) WHICH DISTRACTS DIOMEDES AND WHACKS HIM OVER THE FUCKING HEAD. BECAUSE THAT'S WHAT HERACLES DOES BEST.

HE THEN FEEDS DIOMEDES TO THE HORSES AND LEADS THEM AWAY. HERACLES SERIOUSLY HAD A FUCKING WAY WITH ANIMALS. HE'S JUST LUCKY THERE WASN'T AN ANCIENT GREEK RSPCA.

THE LABOURS OF HERACLES: IX - HIPPOLYTA'S GIRDLE

EURYSTHEUS' SPOILED LITTLE BRAT WANTS A NEW FUCKING BELT. SHE WANTS THE AMAZON QUEEN HIPPOLYTA'S BITCHING BELT. SO HERACLES HAS TO GO AND GET IT.

THE AMAZONS ARE LIKE THE SCARIEST FEMINISTS YOU WILL EVER FUCKING SEE, PLUS THEY ARE THE CHILDREN OF INCEST (ARES AND HIS DAUGHTER. EW.) BESIDES THAT THEY ARE TOTAL BAD-ASS MOTHERFUCKERS.

WHEN HERACLES ARRIVES AT THEIR CITY, HIPPOLYTA JUST FALLS CRAZY IN LOVE WITH HIM. MUST BE BECAUSE HE FUCKING LIFTS. SHE'S GOING TO JUST GIVE HIM THE BELT, BUT HERA FINDS OUT AND DECIDES THAT'S JUST TOO FUCKING EASY. SO SHE SPREADS SOME BITCHY RUMOUR ABOUT HERACLES BEING A TOTAL DICKBAG AROUND THE AMAZONS, WHICH IS PRETTY BELIEVABLE BECAUSE HERACLES IS A DICK TO EVERYONE ELSE. SO THEY DECIDE HE LOOKS LIKE A BIT OF A CRAZY WIFE-KILLING ASSHOLE AND ATTACK HIM.

SO HE FUCKING KILLS ALL OF THEIR LEADERS AND JUST TOOK THE GIRDLE FROM HIPPOLYTA'S STILL-WARM CORPSE. ONCE AGAIN, THE STORY ENDS WITH HERACLES GENERALLY BEING A SHITTY HUMAN BEING.

THE LABOURS OF HERACLES: X - THE CATTLE OF GERYON

GERYON IS THIS TOTALLY FUCKED UP GUY WITH THREE BODIES, THREE HEADS AND SIX ARMS ALL STUCK TOGETHER. HOW THE FUCK DOES HE BUY CLOTHES? ANYWAY, HE HAS SOME FANCY ASS CATTLE THAT HERACLES HAS TO STEAL (YOU'RE PROBABLY NOTICING A BIT OF A FUCKING THEME HERE). ON HIS WAY TO GERYON HERACLES GETS PRETTY FUCKING DISTRACTED, AND ENDS UP CREATING THE ROCK OF GIBRALTAR AND DOING ALL SORTS OF OTHER FLASHY BULLSHIT.

FINALLY HERACLES ROCKS UP AT GERYON'S FARM, AND THEN FUCKING BEATS HIS HERDSMAN AND FAITHFUL DOG TO A BLOODY DEATH. HERACLES JUST GETS GERYON TO STAND SIDEWAYS ON AND FUCKING SHOOTS THAT BITCH THROUGH ALL THREE BODIES. BUT DON'T FUCKING WORRY - HIS BLOOD TURNS INTO A CHERRY TREE. THIS IS FUCKING NORMAL IN MYTHOLOGY, OK.

ONCE AGAIN, HERACLES KILLS EVERYONE. WHAT A FUCKING SHITBUCKET.

THE LABOURS OF HERACLES: XI - THE APPLES OF THE HESPERIDES

HERACLES ORGINALLY HAS TO DO ONLY TEN LABOURS, BUT BECAUSE MR ASSHOLE EURYSTHEUS DISCOUNTED TWO AND FIVE, WHICH IS COMPLETE BULLSHIT, HE HAS TO DO TWO FUCKING MORE. IT'S FUCKING LUCKY THAT THESE ARE THE MOST FUCKING SYMBOLIC ONES, ISN'T IT.

EURYSTHEUS TELLS HERACLES TO STEAL SOME MOTHERFUCKING MAGIC APPLES FROM THE GARDEN OF THE HESPERIDES, OH, AND THESE MAGICAL FRUITS BELONG TO HERA. OUCH. HERACLES THEN GETS FUCKING CONFUSED BECAUSE HE DOESN'T KNOW WHO HE COULD BEAT UP THIS TIME, AND THAT'S ABOUT THE EXTENT OF THE SHIT HE CAN DO. SO HE ASKS MR KNOW-IT-ALL SEA DEITY NEREUS FOR SOME FUCKING ADVICE (HE HAS TO CATCH THIS GUY BY HUGGING HIM TO THE GROUND FIRST, IN A SUSPICIOUSLY HOMOEROTIC WAY).

NEREUS TELLS HIM TO CHEAT AND GET FUCKING ATLAS (THE SKY CARRYING GUY) TO STEAL THEM FOR HIM, BECAUSE POOR ICKLE HERACLES COULDN'T POSSIBLY SLAY THE FUCKING HUNDRED HEADED DRAGON THAT GUARDS THE APPLES ALONE. LONG STORY SHORT - HERACLES SHOOTS THE DRAGON, GETS THAT MOTHERFUCKER ATLAS TO STEAL THE APPLES THEN JUST SCREWS HIM OVER AND TRICKS HIM INTO HOLDING THE SKY AGAIN. GREAT, THREE MAGIC APPLES. OH BUT ATHENA MAKES HERACLES FUCKING GIVE THEM BACK TO HERA, BECAUSE APPARENTLY STEALING IS ILLEGAL, MOTHERFUCKERS.

THE LABOURS OF HERACLES: XII - THE CAPTURE OF CERBERUS

HERACLES GOES DOWN TO THE FUCKING UNDERWORLD TO STEAL ITS GUARD-DOG. YOU'RE REALLY NOT FUCKING SUPPOSED TO DO THAT (AND GET BACK). BUT HERACLES JUST FROWNS AT THE FERRYMAN AND HE'S SO FUCKING SCARED HE LETS HIM IN.

HERACLES IS FUCKING STUPID AND A BIT OF A SHIT THIEF, SO HE GOES AND JUST FUCKING ASKS HADES AND PERSEPHONE FOR THEIR DOG. "SURE BRO, IF YOU CAN FUCKING CATCH IT WITHOUT USING YOUR WEAPONS". SO HERACLES JUST STRANGLES THE FUCKING DOGGIE AND DRAGS IT BACK TO EURYSTHEUS. THEN HE KILLS EURYSTHEUS' KIDS AS A FINAL SCREW-YOU. AS WE'VE SAID BEFORE, HERACLES IS A DICK.

INCIDENTALLY, CERBERUS' NAME SEEMS TO FUCKING DERIVE FROM A PROTO-INDO-EUROPEAN WORD MEANING SPOTTED. HADES FUCKING CALLS HIS BADASS GUARD-DOG 'SPOT'...

HERACLES HAS KINKY FUN

HERACLES IS INVOLVED IN A FUCK-TONNE OF SHENANIGANS THAT, LONG STORY SHORT, END IN HIM GOING CRAZY, KILLING HIS BEST BRO AND TRYING TO BREAK DELPHI.

AN ORACLE TELLS HIM THE ONLY WAY HE CAN MAKE UP FOR THIS SHIT IS TO BE A SLAVE FOR THREE YEARS. HE'S SOLD TO OMPHALE, A LYDIAN QUEEN. OMPHALE MAKES HIM SWAP CLOTHES WITH HER AND THEN THEY FUCK. KINKY.

ONE TIME PAN CREEPS INTO THEIR BEDROOM, SEES SOMEONE IN A DRESS AND THINKS IT'S A LADY. BEING PAN, HE GETS KINDA HORNY, BUT THEN HERACLES LIFTS UP HIS DRESS. PAN IS STUNNED AT HIS GREAT BIG DICK, AND HERACLES BEATS THE CRAP OUT OF HIM (WITH HIS CLUB, PRESUMABLY. OR POSSIBLY HIS DICK).

OMPHALE MAKES HERACLES DO A BUNCH OF REALL STUPID BULLSHIT, LIKE CATCHING SOME ANNOYING DWARVES CALLED THE CERCOPES. HE TIES THOSE LITTLE FUCKERS UPSIDE DOWN TO STOP THEM RUNNING, BUT THEN THEY CAN SEE UP HIS SEXY DRESS. HERACLES HAS A SUPER TANNED ASS FROM RUNNING AROUND NAKED, SO THEY JUST FUCKING LAUGH AT HIM AND CALL HIM "BLACK-BUTT". HERACLES ALSO FINDS THIS FUCKING HILARIOUS AND LET THEM GO.

HERACLES HAS A FUCK TONNE OF KIDS WITH OMPHALE, BUT EVENTUALLY FUCKS OFF BACK TO GREECE TO MARRY ANOTHER GIRL. AS STATED BEFORE, HERACLES IS A FUCK-NOZZLE.

HERACLES GETS (ANOTHER) GIRL

AFTER HERACLES' WEIRD BDSM FLING WITH OMPHALE, HE'S LOOKING FOR ANOTHER GIRL. DEIANEIRA IS A SINGLE LADY, ALSO A DAUGHTER OF DIONYSUS. SO BASICALLY A CRAZY PARTY QUEEN. FUCKING PERFECT.

DEIANEIRA'S ONLY OTHER SUITOR IS SOME UGLY SHAPESHIFTING RIVER FUCKER, SO NOT MUCH COMPETITION. INITIALLY ACHELOUS, THE RIVER DUDE, CALLS HERACLES' MOTHER A SLUT AND SAYS HE ISN'T A SON OF ZEUS. BAD MOVE MOTHERFUCKER. SHIT ESCALATES AND ACHELOUS TURNS INTO A BULL. HERACLES RIPS HIS FUCKING HORN OFF AND MARRIES DEIANEIRA. EVERYTHING IS HAPPY.

THEN ONE DAY THE COUPLE ARE TRAVELLING AND THEY COME TO A RIVER. SOME SUSPICIOUS CENTAUR FUCKER NESSUS OFFERS TO CARRY DEIANEIRA ACROSS THE RIVER WHILE HERACLES SWIMS. HERACLES AGREES BECAUSE HE'S A FUCKING IDIOT. THE CREEPY CENTAUR FUCKS OFF WITH DEIANEIRA AND TRIES TO RAPE HER.

HERACLES SAVES THE DAY AND BEATS THE SHIT OUT OF NESSUS, BUT THEN THE CREEPY FUCKER TELLS DEIANEIRA A FUN RECIPE FOR KEEPING HERACLES FAITHFUL: MIX SOME OF HIS CENTAUR CUM WITH HIS BLOOD AND APPLY TO HERACLES' CLOTHES. WHAT A GREAT FUCKING IDEA. WHEN DEIANEIRA TRIES THIS, IT BURNS ALL OF HERACLES' FUCKING FLESH OFF. WHAT A SHITTY IDEA. BUT HERACLES THEN BECOMES A GOD AND MARRIES HIS HALF-SISTER HEBE SO ALL IS GOOD IN THE MOTHERFUCKING 'HOOD.

HERACLES FUCKS UP TROY

LAOMEDON, THE FUCKING KING OF TROY, PROMISES TO PAY FOR THE GODS HELP WITH BUILDING CITY WALLS WITH HIS FANCY HORSES (GIVEN TO TROY IN EXCHANGE FOR ZEUS KIDNAPPING GANYMEDE, KEEP UP), BUT HE'S A LYING ASSHOLE. IN REVENGE, APOLLO SENDS TROY A MOTHERFUCKING PLAGUE, AND POSEIDON SENDS A BIG-ASS SEA MONSTER WHICH CAN ONLY POSSIBLY BE STOPPED BY GIVING IT A PRINCESS. VERY FUCKING ORIGINAL. CONVENIENTLY PRINCESS HESIONE IS ON HAND... HERACLES HEARS ABOUT THIS AND SHOWS UP, SAYING HE'LL KILL THE MONSTROUS FUCKER IF LAOMEDON GIVES HIM THOSE FUCKING HORSES. LAOMEDON SAYS SURE THING (HERACLES IS A BIT OF AN IDIOT).

HERACLES' BATTLE PLAN IS TO GET EATEN BY THE MONSTER, AND FOR THREE DAYS HE FIGHTS IT FROM THE INSIDE BECAUSE HE IS ONE BAD-ASS MOTHER-FUCKER. EVENTUALLY HE CUTS ITS TONGUE OFF AND EVERYTHING IS GROOVY. BUT OF COURSE LAOMEDON DOESN'T GIVE HERACLES THE HORSES, BECAUSE HE IS A COMPLETE ASSHOLE (ALSO THESE ARE SOME MIGHTY FINE EQUINES).

HERACLES GOES FUCKING CRAZY BECAUSE HE'S HERACLES AND THAT'S WHAT HE DOES. HE AND A SMALL GANG TRASH TROY, KILL LAOMEDON AND MOST OF THE IMPORTANT FUCKERS. THIS TOOK AGAMEMNON AND FRIENDS 10 FUCKING YEARS. HERACLES GETS SHIT DONE. THE ONLY SURVIVORS ARE THE PRINCESS, HESIONE, AND HER BROTHER PODARCES (WHO CHANGED HIS NAME TO PRIAM FOR LEGAL REASONS).

A STORY ABOUT BUTTS

ON ONE OF THESEUS' ADVENTURES, HE FUCKS OFF DOWN TO THE FUCKING UNDERWORLD TO KIDNAP PERSEPHONE (YOU'D THINK SHE'D BE PRETTY FUCKING DONE WITH BEING KIDNAPPED BY NOW).

WHEN HE GETS THERE, HE AWKWARDLY BUMPS INTO HADES, WHO JUST SAYS "TAKE A FUCKING SEAT". THESEUS TAKES SAID FUCKING SEAT AND PLONKS HIS BUTT DOWN. AND GETS FUCKING STUCK TO THE CHAIR FOR FUCKING AGES.

BUT WHEN HERACLES COMES BY AND SEES THESEUS SITTING THERE LIKE A STUPID FUCKING LEMON, HE GIVES HIM A HAND UP. BUT REMEMBER THAT HERACLES IS BOTH FUCKING STRONG AND A COMPLETE ASSHOLE. SO HE LITERALLY RIPS THESEUS FROM THE CHAIR, AND LEAVES PART OF HIS BUTT STUCK TO THE CHAIR.

THESEUS THEN GOES BACK TO BE AN ANCESTOR OF ATHENS. THIS IS OF COURSE WHY ATHENIANS SUPPOSEDLY HAVE FUCKING SMALL BUTTS.

SCIENCE, MOTHERFUCKERS.

TIRESIAS: THE SASSIEST MOTHERFUCKER IN THE MYTHOLOGICAL WORLD

TIRESIAS IS EVERYONE'S FUCKING FAVOURITE OLD MAN. HAVING TROUBLE WITH YOUR FUCKING FAMILY? ASK TIRESIAS. NEED DIRECTIONS TO GET HOME? ASK THIS ASSHOLE, EVEN IF HE'S   DEAD. HE'S AWESOME BECAUSE NOT ONLY CAN HE TELL THE FUTURE AND IS ONE SNARKY MOTHERFUCKER, HE ALSO HAS ONE OF THE COOLEST FUCKING ORIGIN STORIES.

ONE TIME TIRESIAS IS WALKING IN THE COUNTRYSIDE NEAR THEBES, AND SEES SOME SNAKES FUCKING. BEING THE COMPLETE VIOLENT ASSHOLE EVERYONE IN THE MYTHOLOGICAL WORLD IS, HE BEATS THE FEMALE SNAKE TO DEATH WITH A STICK. THEN HE TURNS INTO A WOMAN (THIS SHIT HAPPENS A LOT OK). BEING A WOMAN HE NATURALLY SLEEPS WITH EVERYONE AND HAS SEVERAL KIDS. THAT'S JUST WHAT PEOPLE DO IN THIS SITUATION IN THE ANCIENT WORLD. FEM!TIRESIAS FINDS TWO MORE SNAKES FUCKING, SO THIS TIME SQUISHES THE MALE ONE (TIRESIAS JUST REALLY HATES SNAKES), AND BECOMES A FUCKING MAN AGAIN.

HERA ARGUES WITH ZEUS ABOUT WHETHER MEN OR WOMEN GET MORE PLEASURE FROM SEX. SHE'S PRETTY FUCKING PISSED OFF THAT ZEUS IS CHEATING ALL THE FUCKING TIME, BUT HIS EXCUSE IS THAT ALL THE YOUNG GIRLS HE WAS BASICALLY RAPING REALLY FUCKING LOVE IT. HERA THINKS OTHERWISE (AS USUAL). TO SOLVE THE FUCKING ARGUMENT THEY ASK TIRESIAS, BECAUSE HE KNOWS BASICALLY FUCKING EVERYTHING.

TIRESIAS AGREES WITH ZEUS, SO HERA FUCKING BLINDS HIM. BECAUSE OF THE WHOLE 'ONE GOD'S POWER CAN'T UNDO ANOTHER' BULLSHIT, ZEUS CAN ONLY GIVE TIRESIAS MOTHERFUCKING INNER SIGHT, SO HE CAN SEE THE FUTURE (WHETHER HIS SNARKINESS COMES WITH THIS WE DON'T FUCKING KNOW)

MOTHERFUCKING OEDIPUS

ONE DAY, LAIUS AND JOCASTA (KING AND QUEEN OF THEBES) HEAR A REALLY SHITTY PROPHECY SAYING THAT LAIUS WILL BE KILLED BY HIS OWN SON. SO WHAT DO THEY DO WITH THEIR NEW BABY? THAT'S RIGHT. DUMP HIM ON A FUCKING MOUNTAIN. BECAUSE THAT WORKS OUT SO FUCKING WELL FOR EVERYONE ELSE THAT DOES IT. OH, AND THEY STAB A FUCKING GREAT METAL PIN THROUGH HIS FEET, BECAUSE DUMPING BABIES ON MOUNTAINS JUST ISN'T EVIL ENOUGH.

NATURALLY THE BABY DOESN'T DIE. GREEK BABIES ARE ALL FUCKING MAGIC AND INDESTRUCTIBLE. THIS IS JUST HOW LIFE WORKS. A SHEPHERD PICKS HIM UP AND GOES LOOKING FOR PEOPLE IN NEED OF KIDS. SOON ENOUGH BABY OEDIPUS HAS BEEN GIVEN TO POLYBUS AND MEROPE, THE KING AND QUEEN OF CORINTH, WHO DON'T SEEM TO CARE THAT THEY'VE JUST BEEN GIVEN A MAIMED, BLOODSTAINED BABY BY SOME CREEPY MOTHERFUCKER THEY'VE NEVER SEEN BEFORE.

YEARS LATER, OEDIPUS HEARS THE SAME FUCKING PROPHECY, AND RUNS AWAY FROM HOME IN ORDER TO NOT BE NEAR HIS DAD. WHAT A FUCKING IDIOT.

MEANWHILE, THEBES HAS A MONSTER PROBLEM. THERE'S A MOTHERFUCKING SPHINX HANGING ABOUT OUTSIDE THE WALLS AND BEING REALLY ANNOYING. IN THIS CASE ANNOYING MEANS KILLING PEOPLE. THE SPHINX IS A FUCKING HORRIBLE MONSTER WITH THE BODY OF A LION, THE FACE OF A WOMAN, THE WINGS OF AN EAGLE AND A LOVE OF SHITTY RIDDLES. TO GET RID OF IT, LAIUS SETS OFF ON A TRIP TO DELPHI TO ASK FOR ADVICE FROM THE ORACLE.

ON HIS WAY, HE RUNS INTO OEDIPUS AND TRIES TO SHOVE HIM OFF THE ROAD. OEDIPUS' REACTION IS PERFECTLY NORMAL. HE BEATS HIM AND ALL HIS MEN TO DEATH WITH A STICK BECAUSE, LIKE ALL GREEK HEROES, OEDIPUS IS A DICK. UNAWARE THAT HE JUST MURDERED HIS OWN FATHER, OEDIPUS HEADS TO THEBES.

THEN HE GETS TO THEBES, MURDERS THE FUCKING SPHINX (OK WE LIED ABOUT THE ANIMAL ABUSE) AND GETS PROCLAIMED KING. AND THEN HE MARRIES THE QUEEN. WHO'S HIS MUM. BUT NEITHER OF THEM KNOW THAT.

OEDIPUS IS MOTHERFUCKING STUPID (NO WE WILL NEVER GET TIRED OF THAT JOKE), AND THINGS ARE ONLY GOING TO GET WORSE.

YEARS PASS. OEDIPUS HAS KIDS. YEAH, WITH HIS MUM. THEY'RE GOING TO HAVE PRETTY SHITTY LIVES. A FUCKING PLAGUE ARRIVES IN THEBES, AND OEDIPUS SENDS HIS BROTHER-IN-LAW/UNCLE CREON TO FIND OUT WHAT HE SHOULD DO TO FIX IT.

CREON COMES BACK AND SAYS THAT IT'S ALL BECAUSE OF SOME MURDEROUS WANKER IN THE TOWN AND THE MURDERER NEEDS TO BE THROWN OUT. OEDIPUS CALLS ALL SORTS OF FUCKING CURSES DOWN ON THE MURDERER, NOT REALISING THAT IT'S HIM.

HE CALLS TIRESIAS, THE BLIND SEER (MORE ON HIM LATER) AND ASKS WHAT TO DO. TIRESIAS, WHO IS ONE SNARKY MOTHERFUCKER, SAYS "HA HA I KNOW SOMETHING YOU DON'T KNOW. GIVE UP. FUCK OFF. YOU DON'T WANT TO KNOW." OEDIPUS SHOUTS AT HIM AND ACCUSES HIM OF ALL SORTS OF SHIT. TIRESIAS PULLS A FACE AT HIM, TELLS HIM HE'S THE MURDERER, AND FUCKS OFF.

JOCASTA SHOWS UP AND RAMBLES ABOUT HOW LAIUS DIED, AT WHICH POINT OEDIPUS GOES "OH SHIT. MAYBE I DID IT." AND STARTS TO PANIC.

JOCASTA TELLS HIM ALL PROPHECIES ARE BULLSHIT AND EXPLAINS THE ONE ABOUT HOW LAIUS WOULD BE KILLED BY HIS SON AND HOW THAT TOTALLY DIDN'T HAPPEN.

THEN, AFTER SHOUTING AT A FEW SHEPHERDS AND BEING SO FUCKING STUPID AND OBLIVIOUS TO EVERYTHING THAT HE

DOESN'T REALISE WHAT HE'S DONE, OEDIPUS REALISES HIS WIFE/MUM'S GONE. SHE'S WORKED IT OUT. SHE KNOWS SHE SLEPT WITH HER OWN FUCKING SON WHO ALSO KILLED HIS DAD.

JOCASTA'S PRETTY FUCKING UPSET, AND HANGS HERSELF. OEDIPUS FINALLY WORKS OUT WHAT HE'S DONE, RUNS TO SAVE HER, GETS THERE A BIT TOO LATE, AND STABS OUT HIS OWN EYES IN DISTRESS.

OEDIPUS IS NOW BLIND AND COVERED IN SHITLOADS OF BLOOD. HE FUCKS OFF OUT OF TOWN INTO EXILE, LEAVING HIS KIDS TO BE LOOKED AFTER BY THEIR UNCLE/GREAT UNCLE. CREON IS SHIT WITH KIDS. REALLY, REALLY SHIT. SO THAT'S IT. CHEERFUL STORY. IT'S GOT INCEST, MURDER, SUICIDE AND STABBING OUT OF EYES. IT'S FUCKING GREAT.

ANTIGONE (A.K.A. MOTHERFUCKING OEDIPUS II)

A FEW YEARS AFTER THE FUCKING INCEST INCIDENT, OEDIPUS' CHILDREN GROW UP WITH THEIR UNCLE/GREAT UNCLE CREON TRYING TO PARENT THEM. HE'S A PRETTY SHIT PARENT. SO SHIT, IN FACT, THAT POLYNICES (ONE OF OEDIPUS' SONS) GOES INTO REVOLT. HE MARCHES ON THEBES WITH A FUCKING ARMY, AND HIS BROTHER ETEOCLES COMES OUT TO STOP HIM. LONG STORY SHORT: THEY BOTH KILL EACH OTHER AND EVERYONE'S FUCKING MISERABLE.

ETEOCLES GETS BURIED LIKE A HERO, BUT WHEN IT COMES TO POLYNICES CREON SAYS "HA HA FUCK NO" AND INSISTS THAT HE HAS TO BE LEFT OUT IN THE SUN TO GO RUNNY RATHER THAN GETTING A DECENT FUCKING BURIAL. HIS SISTER ANTIGONE IS UNDERSTANDABLY PRETTY FUCKING UPSET BY THIS. HIS OTHER SISTER ISMENE DOESN'T GIVE A SHIT.

ONE NIGHT, ANTIGONE SNEAKS OUT OF THE CITY AND STARTS BURYING HER BROTHER. SHE ONLY GETS HALF WAY, THOUGH, BEFORE THE GUARDS SHOW UP AND SHE HAS TO FUCK OFF AT HIGH SPEED.

CREON HEARS ABOUT THIS AND IS FUCKING FURIOUS. HE DEMANDS MORE GUARDS SO HE CAN FIND OUT WHO DID IT.

THE NEXT NIGHT, ANTIGONE SNEAKS OUT AGAIN AND FINISHES THE JOB. THEN THE FUCKING GUARDS CATCH HER AND DRAG HER TO CREON.

THEY SHOUT AT EACH OTHER A BIT AND THEN CREON SENTENCES HER TO DEATH. HE'S A REALLY SHIT PARENT.

WHEN ANTIGONE'S FIANCE HAEMON (WHO'S ALSO CREON'S SON AND THEREFORE HER COUSIN AND ALSO A DIFFERENT SORT OF COUSIN [INCEST MAKES THIS BULLSHIT PRETTY FUCKING COMPLICATED. DON'T DO IT KIDS.]) FINDS OUT HIS DAD'S JUST SENTENCED ANTIGONE TO DEATH, HE'S FUCKING

FURIOUS. THEY HAVE A SHOUTING MATCH AND HAEMON RUNS OFF IN TEARS.

THEN TIRESIAS, THE SNARKIEST MOTHERFUCKER IN ALL OF GREECE, SHOWS UP AND TELLS CREON TO STOP BEING A DICK. CREON, HAVING NO RESPECT FOR ANNOYING OLD BLIND MEN, TELLS HIM TO FUCK OFF. TIRESIAS SNARKS AT HIM FOR A BIT AND THEN FUCKS OFF.

ALL THAT HAPPENS A FEW TIMES, AND THEN CREON SUDDENLY THINKS "OH SHIT. MAYBE SHE SHOULDN'T DIE." AND RUNS OFF TO THE CAVE WHERE HE'D ORDERED HER TO BE FUCKING BURIED ALIVE. GREAT PARENTING THERE.

WHEN HE GETS THERE, SHE'S HANGED HERSELF IN DESPAIR. HAEMON SEES THIS, GRABS A SWORD, SCREAMS A BIT, RUNS AT HIS DAD AND THEN STABS HIMSELF IN THE STOMACH. IT'S NOT A GOOD DAY FOR CREON, AND IT'S ABOUT TO GET EVEN FUCKING WORSE.

WHEN HE GETS HOME, CARRYING THE BODY OF HIS SON, HE DISCOVERS THAT HIS WIFE'S FOUND OUT WHAT HAPPENED AND KILLED HERSELF. CREON'S LEFT SITTING THERE IN A HOUSE FULL OF CORPSES. IT'S A REALLY FUCKING SHIT DAY FOR EVERYONE.

ATALANTA IS A BADASS MOTHERFUCKER WITH FRUIT PROBLEMS

FUCK YEAH BADASS GREEK LADY POWER!

ATALANTA'S FATHER WANTS A SON SO HE LEAVES HER ON A MOUNTAIN TO DIE. OF COURSE SHE HAS SPECIAL FUCKING ABANDONED BABY POWERS AND SURVIVES LONG ENOUGH TO BE RESCUED. BY A SHEPHERD? NO. BY A BEAR. A FUCKING BEAR ADOPTS HER. SHE GROWS UP TO BE AN EPIC HUNTRESS AND HAVE VARIOUS ADVENTURES, ONE INVOLVING SOME BOAR-HUNT WITH THIS EPIC DICK MELEAGER WHO'S OBSESSED WITH HER AND WON'T LET IT GO. THEN HE DIES SLOWLY AND HORRIBLY, SO EVERYTHING'S FINE.

HER SEXIST-ASS DADDY (THE REAL ONE, NOT THE BEAR) EVENTUALLY RECLAIMS HER AND TRIES TO MAKE HER MARRY A VARIETY OF DICKS. SHE SAYS NO FUCKING WAY, UNLESS ONE OF THEM CAN BEAT HER IN A RACE (SHE WANTS A MAN AS SWIFT AS A COURSING RIVER OK). TONNES OF SUITORS ARE TOO SLOW, SO SHE HAS THEM FUCKING KILLED. SEE, EVEN THE LADIES IN GREEK MYTHOLOGY ARE DICKS. FINALLY, HIPPOMENES DECIDES HE WANTS TO HAVE THIS BADASS AS A WIFE, SO HE CHEATS BY ASKING APHRODITE FOR HELP. SHE GIVES HIM SOME APPLES.

INSTEAD OF MAKING A FRUIT SALAD, HE JUST CHUCKS APPLES AT ATALANTA AS SHE SPRINTS AWAY, AND BECAUSE APPLES ARE SO FUCKING DISTRACTING, SHE LOSES AND HAS TO MARRY THE SNEAKY BASTARD. OH AND THEN THEY HAVE SEX IN ZEUS' TEMPLE AND HE TURNS THEM INTO LIONS. FUCKING BADASS LIONS.

FUN GREEK FACT: THROWING AN APPLE AT SOMEONE IS A FUN WAY TO PROPOSE - IF THEY CATCH IT THEN THEY FUCKING LOVE YOU BACK, IF NOT, THEY GET INJURED AND WILL PROBABLY DECLARE YOU A MORTAL ENEMY. IT'S A WIN FUCKING WIN SITUATION.

CAN WE JUST FUCKING TALK ABOUT PRIAPUS?

BRACE YOURSELVES, MOTHERFUCKERS.

PRIAPUS IS THE GREEK/ROMAN GOD OF FERTILITY, GOATS AND FUCKING BEES (INTERPRET THAT HOW YOU WANT). HE'S ALSO EFFECTIVELY THE GOD OF MOTHERFUCKING BONERS, AND HE IS USUALLY REPRESENTED WITH A STUPID-ASS HAT AND A HUGE FUCKING ERECTION.

THE BEST FUCKING STORY ABOUT PRIAPUS IS WHEN HE'S AT A PARTY WITH HIS (POSSIBLE) DADDY DIONYSUS, SHIT TONNES OF SATYRS AND HOT NYMPH LADIES. EVERYONE GETS SERIOUSLY FUCKING DRUNK AND EVENTUALLY GOES TO SLEEP. EXCEPT PRIAPUS, WHO THINKS THIS WOULD BE A GREAT TIME TO TRY AND RAPE ONE OF THE NYMPHS, WHO HAD CLEARLY TOLD HIM NO EARLIER IN THE EVENING.

HE CREEPS OVER TO HER, BONER OUT AS USUAL, BUT THEN A FUCKING DONKEY SEES HIM AND STARTS BEING A NOISY ASSHOLE. THE NYMPH WAKES UP AND NATURALLY RUNS THE FUCK AWAY FROM CREEPY-ASS PRIAPUS. HE THEN GETS SUPER MAD WITH THE DONKEY AND BEATS IT TO FUCKING DEATH WITH HIS BONER. YES. SERIOUSLY.

MORAL OF THE STORY? JUST DON'T BE FUCKING PRIAPUS. OR A DONKEY. JUST DON'T BE INVOLVED WITH FUCKING MYTHOLOGY.

APHRODITE

THE STORY GOES THAT ONE TIME, OURANOS (THE FUCKING SKY) IS COMING (EHE) DOWN TO EARTH TO FUCK GAIA (THE FUCKING EARTH). THE TITAN KRONOS (ALSO THEIR FUCKING SON), BEING THE TOTAL ASSHOLE HE IS, DOESN'T WANT TO HAVE MORE ASSHOLE SIBLINGS, AND HAS THE MOST LOGICAL FUCKING REACTION TO SEEING HIS PARENTS FUCK: HE CUTS HIS DAD'S GENITALS OFF WITH HIS BADASS SCYTHE.

HE THEN THROWS SAID GENITALS INTO THE FUCKING SEA. FUCK RECYCLING. TO EVERYONE'S SURPRISE THE SEA STARTS FOAMING AND THEN APHRODITE SPRINGS OUT MAJESTICALLY, LOOKING AS FUCKING FABULOUS AS YOU WOULD EXPECT THE GODDESS OF LOVE AND BEAUTY TO BE.

APHRODITE IS THEN EVENTUALLY MARRIED OFF TO HEPHAESTUS, BUT HE'S KINDA LIMPY AND SAD SO SHE JUST FUCKS OFF AND HAS SHIT TONNES OF AFFAIRS. HER MOST FAMOUS ONE IS WITH ARES, HOT ASS GOD OF WAR. HEPHAESTUS IS PRETTY FUCKING PISSED OFF ABOUT THIS SO HE MAKES A BOOBY-TRAPPED BED AND LEAVES IT FOR APHRODITE AND ARES TO FUCK ON. THEY'RE ABOUT TO GET GOING WHEN HEPHAESTUS PRESSES THE FUCKING LEVER AND THE COUPLE AERE TRAPPED NAKED IN GOLD CHAINS. FUCKING KINKY. THEN ALL THE OTHER GODS COME OVER TO FUCKING LAUGH AT THEM (AND BE JEALOUS OF ARES).

MINOS HAS A BAD EXPERIENCE WITH A COW

ONE DAY, KING MINOS, WHO IS A BIT OF A DICK AND ALSO THE KING OF KNOSSOS ON THE ISLAND OF CRETE, HAS A REALLY FUCKING STUPID IDEA.

HE INSULTS POSEIDON. THAT'S RIGHT, THE MOTHERFUCKING SEA GOD. AND POSEIDON IS NOT SOMEBODY WHO LIKES BEING FUCKING INSULTED. AT ALL. SO WHAT DOES HE DO? HE MAKES MINOS' WIFE PASIPHAE FALL IN LOVE WITH A SACRED BULL, OF COURSE. WHAT A FUCKING DICK.

PASIPHAE, NOT BEING A COMPLETE FUCKING IDIOT, REALISES THAT FALLING IN LOVE WITH A BULL IS A BIT OF A PROBLEM, AS KINKY COW SEX IS A BIT IMPRACTICAL AND ALSO THE BULL DOESN'T FANCY HER BACK. FORTUNATELY FOR HER, THOUGH, HER HUSBAND HAS A PET INVENTOR HE KEEPS IN A FUCKING BOX. SHE ASKS DAEDALUS NICELY, AND HE MAKES HER A METAL COW SUIT. THAT'S RIGHT, HE MAKES HER A COSTUME SO SHE CAN PRETEND TO BE A REALLY FUCKING SEXY COW. THEN SHE HAS SEX WITH THE SACRED BULL. MINOS IS PROBABLY PRETTY FUCKING DISTURBED BY ALL THIS HORRIBLE BULLSHIT.

BUT IT DOESN'T STOP THERE. OH NO. THE BULL GETS HER PREGNANT, AND SHE GIVES BIRTH TO A HALF MAN, HALF COW MONSTER.

NATURALLY, MINOS LOOKS AT IT AND JUST GOES "WHAT THE FUCK IS THIS THING?" AND HAS IT LOCKED UP IN A MAZE UNDER THE PALACE. THE SENSIBLE THING TO DO WOULD HAVE BEEN TO KILL IT, BUT MINOS IS A FUCKING IDIOT.

THESEUS JUST REALLY FUCKING HATES COWS

KING MINOS OF CRETE HAS AN ANGRY COW MONSTER LOCKED UP IN A MAZE UNDER THE PALACE, SO NATURALLY HE NEEDS TO FEED THE LITTLE FUCKER.

WHAT DO COW MONSTERS EAT? NO, NOT GRASS. FUCKING PEOPLE.

FORTUNATELY, THE MINOANS ARE PIRATES. YES, ACTUAL PIRATES. THEY'VE GOT LARGE PARTS OF GREECE IN TERROR OF THEM. SO THEY ASK FOR TRIBUTES FROM ALL THE GREEK STATES. KIND OF LIKE THE HUNGER GAMES, ONLY WITH A REALLY FUCKING HUNGRY MINOTAUR AND NO WINNERS.

ONE YEAR, THESEUS, THE SON OF KING AEGEUS, GETS PICKED TO BE COW FOOD. HE'S FINE WITH THIS SHIT. HIS DAD ISN'T.

THESEUS GETS TO CRETE, AND ARIADNE, THE FUCKING DAUGHTER OF MINOS, THINKS HE'S PRETTY FUCKING HOT AND DECIDES TO SAVE HIM. SHE GIVES HIM A FUCKING PIECE OF STRING AND TELLS HIM TO USE IT TO GET OUT OF THE MAZE, WHICH SOUNDS LIKE BULLSHIT TO THESEUS. THESEUS ISN'T VERY BRIGHT. ACTUALLY, LIKE MOST HEROES, HE'S AS THICK AS A FUCKING BRICK.

IN THE END HE WORKS OUT WHAT TO DO, KILLS THE COW, BACKTRACKS USING THE STRING, KIDNAPS ARIADNE AND SAILS HOME.

HAPPY ENDING? HA, FUCK NO.

EARLIER, HE'D TOLD HIS DAD THAT IF HE WAS ALIVE HE'D PUT UP WHITE SAILS ON THE WAY HOME AND IF HE WAS DEAD HE'D PUT UP BLACK SAILS. OR GET SOMEONE ELSE TO PUT THEM UP, BECAUSE HE'D BE FUCKING DEAD.

WHAT DOES HE DO? YEAH, THAT'S FUCKING RIGHT. HE FORGETS TO PUT UP THE WHITE SAILS. HIS DAD THINKS HE'S DEAD AND

THROWS HIMSELF OFF A CLIFF AND DIES. THESEUS IS FUCKING STUPID.

AND IS THAT THE ONLY THING HE FORGETS? FUCK NO, HE FORGETS ARIADNE TOO. THAT'S RIGHT, HE LEAVES HER ON A BEACH ON SOME SHITTY LITTLE ISLAND ON HIS WAY HOME. THEN HE MARRIES HER SISTER. WHAT A FUCKING DICK.

DAEDALUS

DAEDALUS REALLY FUCKING LIKES MAKING SHIT. WHEN HE REALISES HIS SHITTY LITTLE NEPHEW PERDIX IS BETTER AT MAKING SHIT THAN HIM, HE FUCKING KILLS HIM. ATHENS DOESN'T REALLY LIKE MURDEROUS FUCKERS, SO HE HAS TO FUCK OFF WITH HIS SON ICARUS AND LIVE SOMEWHERE ELSE.

KING MINOS OF CRETE IS IN THE MARKET FOR SOMEONE WHO INVENTS SHIT, BECAUSE HIS WIFE HAS JUST HAD THIS FUCKED-UP COW MONSTER THING AND HE NEEDS SOMEWHERE TO HIDE IT. MINOS HIRES IN DAEDALUS TO BUILD HIM A WHOLE FUCKING LABYRINTH, THEN HE JUST WON'T LET HIM LEAVE BECAUSE DAEDALUS IS TOO FULL OF FUCKING SECRETS TO FREE. NATURALLY DAEDALUS IS PISSED AT MINOS, SO HE HAS NO PROBLEM WITH HELPING THESEUS KILL THE FUCKING MINOTAUR AND START HIS CAREER AS A HERO.

THIS MAKES MINOS EVEN MORE ANGRY BECAUSE NOW HIS FUCKING FREAK-SON IS DEAD AND HIS DAUGHTER KIDNAPPED, SO HE HAS DAEDALUS AND HIS SON ICARUS LOCKED UP IN SOME FUCKING TOWER. AFTER SOME IMPRESSIVE BIRD CATCHING, DAEDALUS HAS A SHIT-TONNE OF FEATHERS AND THE ARTS AND CRAFTS SKILLS NECESSARY TO MAKE FUCKING MASSIVE WINGS FOR HIM AND HIS SON WITHOUT ANYONE NOTICING. FUCKING GENIUS.

THE DAY OF ESCAPE ARRIVES AND DAEDALUS GIVES HIS SON SOME DULL-ASS DAD LECTURE ABOUT SAFE FLYING BLAH BLAH BLAH. ICARUS COMPLETELY IGNORES THIS, THE LITTLE SHIT, AND SO FLIES TOO FUCKING HIGH AND THE SUN MELTS THE WAX HOLDING HIS WINGS TOGETHER. HE FALLS IN THE SEA AND FUCKING DROWNED.

MEANWHILE DAEDALUS FLIES AS FAR AS ITALY/SICILY AND THEN FUCKS AROUND IN THE MEDITERRANEAN FOR A BIT UNTIL HE COMES TO THE PALACE OF SOME FRIENDLY NEIGHBOURHOOD TYRANT. MINOS, HOWEVER, IS ON SOME

FUCKING JAVERT-LIKE HUNT FOR HIS PET INVENTOR, USING SOME SHIT INVOLVING A SHELL BASED PUZZLE TO LURE HIM OUT. EVENTUALLY HE GETS TO THE PALACE WHERE DAEDALUS ISS STAYING, AND OF COURSE DAEDALUS CAN'T RESIST A GOOD FUCKING PUZZLE. LUCKILY THE TYRANT'S DAUGHTERS KINDLY HELP TO FUCKING MURDER MINOS WITH BOILING WATER, SO ALL IS GOOD.

HIPPOLYTUS IS JUST REALLY FUCKING STUPID

IN THE END THESEUS COMES HOME. WITH A BASTARD SON. YEAH, HE RAPED AN AMAZON. WHAT A FUCKING DICK.

HE COMES HOME WITH A BASTARD SON AND A HOT NEW WIFE WHO HAPPENS TO BE THE SISTER OF ARIADNE, WHO GOT LEFT ON A FUCKING ISLAND WHEN THESEUS FORGOT ABOUT HER.

ANYWAY, THESEUS LEAVES TOWN BECAUSE HE KILLED SOMEBODY BECAUSE HE'S FUCKING STUPID. MEANWHILE, HIS SON HIPPOLYTUS IS BEING AN IDIOT. HE'S SWORN OFF WOMEN AND WORSHIPPING APHRODITE IN FAVOUR OF DEVOTING HIMSELF TO ARTEMIS IN A REALLY CREEPY STALKERY WAY.

NEEDLESS TO SAY, APHRODITE IS FUCKING FURIOUS, AND WHEN APHRODITE IS FURIOUS, SHIT GOES DOWN.

APHRODITE DECIDES TO MAKE THESEUS' NEW WIFE (AND THEREFORE HIPPOLYTUS' FUCKING STEPMUM) PHAEDRA FALL IN LOVE WITH HIPPOLYTUS. THAT'S JUST FUCKING WEIRD AND TWISTED AND INCESTUOUS.

HIPPOLYTUS FINDS OUT AND GETS REALLY REALLY UPSET. IT'S UNDERSTANDABLE. HE'S SWORN OFF WOMEN AND SUDDENLY HIS STEPMUM WANTS TO DO HIM.

THEN PHAEDRA FINDS OUT THAT HIPPOLYTUS HAS FOUND OUT THAT SHE FANCIES HIM. THIS IS BEGINNING TO FEEL LIKE A MOTHERFUCKING SHAKESPEAREAN COMEDY, AND NOT ONE OF THE GOOD ONES.

PHAEDRA TAKES THE OBVIOUS COURSE OF ACTION AND KILLS HERSELF, LEAVING A NOTE THAT SAYS THAT HIPPOLYTUS TRIED TO RAPE HER. WHEN THESEUS GETS HOME HE FINDS THIS HORRIBLE MESS AND BANISHES HIPPOLYTUS. SUDDENLY THIS FEELS LESS LIKE A COMEDY AND MORE LIKE A STRING OF HORRIBLE BULLSHIT.

THEN HE CURSES HIPPOLYTUS, AND BECAUSE POSEIDON OWES THESEUS A FAVOUR, THE CURSE MEANS THAT A GIGANTIC MOTHERFUCKING COW COMES OUT OF THE WATER AND TRAMPLES HIM TO DEATH.

THAT'S WHAT YOU GET IF YOU DON'T DO RELIGION PROPERLY. IT'S ALL HIPPOLYTUS' OWN FAULT FOR BEING SUCH A FUCKING IDIOT.

THE WORLD'S SHITTIEST WEDDING GIFT

PROMETHEUS AND EPIMETHEUS ARE TITANS, BUT BECAUSE THEY AREN'T AS BIG ASSHOLES AS THE OTHER TITANS, THE GODS KEEP THEM AROUND AFTER THEY COME TO POWER. ZEUS GIVES THESE BROTHERS THE TASK OF CREATING MANKIND FROM SOME FUCKING MUD.

THEY DO THIS, BUT THEN PROMETHEUS FEELS SORRY FOR HIS CREATIONS BECAUSE HE'S A SHIT ARTIST AND THEY KINDA SUCK AND ARE COLD AND ALWAYS IN THE DARK; THEY DON'T HAVE FIRE. PROMETHEUS THEN STEALS SOME FOR THEM FROM OLYMPUS, BY LIGHTING A FENNEL-STALK. GREEKS ARE FUCKING SPECIFIC OK. ZEUS IS MAJORLY PISSED OFF ABOUT THIS, SO MAKES THE LOGICAL MOVE OF CHAINING PROMETHEUS TO A ROCK AND SETTING A LIVER-HUNGRY EAGLE ON HIM. WHAT A DICKTRUMPET.

BUT ZEUS ISN'T DONE WITH PUNISHING PEOPLE. HE ASKS HEPHAESTUS AND SOME OF THE OTHER GODS TO MAKE THE FIRST WOMAN (YES THE BROTHERS HAD FUCKING FORGOTTEN ABOUT MAKING WOMEN). SHE'S SUPER HOT AND SUPER SNEAKY, AND ALSO MAKES A GREAT GIFT FOR EPIMETHEUS TO MARRY. FOR A WEDDING GIFT, INSTEAD OF JUST FUCKING GIVING THEM A KNIFE-RACK, THROW PILLOWS OR SOME OTHER NORMAL SHIT, ZEUS GIVES THEM A MYSTERIOUS JAR AND TELLS THEM NEVER EVER EVER EVER TO FUCKING OPEN IT.

SO OF COURSE, STRAIGHT AFTER THE WEDDING PARTY, SNEAKY PANDORA GOES AND FUCKING OPENS IT, LIKE THE FOOLISH WOMAN SHE IS. OUT FLIES ALL KINDS OF NASTY SHIT LIKE SUFFERING, COLLEGE FINALS, DEATH, POVERTY AND IRREGULAR VERBS. PANDORA PRESUMABLY SAT AND DID FUCKING NOTHING, BECAUSE SOON THE ONLY THING LEFT WAS HOPE. BECAUSE DEEP DOWN, THAT'S ALL YOU MAJESTIC MOTHER-FUCKERS REALLY HAVE. THE GREEKS GET FUCKING DEEP SOMETIMES...

DOUBLE EGG SURPRISE

LEDA IS QUEEN OF MOTHERFUCKING SPARTA, NEWLY MARRIED TO KING TYNDAREUS AND EVERYTHING IS FUCKING GREAT. ONE DAY SHE STEPS OUTSIDE AND ZEUS SEES HER. WOAH SHIT. BUT IF YOU'RE KING OF THE FUCKING GODS YOU DO NOT DO SUBTLE SEDUCTION, YOU TURN INTO A MASSIVE RAPE-SWAN.

IF YOU BITCHES AREN'T SCARED OF SWANS ALREADY YOU REALLY SHOULD BE. AFTER FUCKING A BIG-ASS SWAN WHO PROBABLY DOESN'T EVEN MENTION HE'S MOTHERFUCKING ZEUS, LEDA GOES BACK TO THE PALACE AND SLEEPS WITH HER HUSBAND TYNDAREUS.

PRESUMABLY EVERYONE IS CONFUSED AS FUCK WHEN NINE MONTHS LATER, LEDA GIVES BIRTH TO NOT ONE BUT TWO MASSIVE EGGS. THIS SHIT WAS DEFINITELY NOT DISCUSSED IN SEX ED CLASS. OUT OF ONE EGG POPS CLYTEMNESTRA AND CASTOR, WHO ARE SOMEHOW TYNDAREUS' KIDS. FROM THE OTHER EGG COMES POLYDEUCES AND SOME BITCH CALLED HELEN (YES THAT HELEN). THERE ARE BABIES EVERYWHERE AND SEEMINGLY TYNDAREUS DOESN'T GIVE A FUCK ABOUT WHAT HIS WIFE HAS PRODUCED BECAUSE HE'S A COOL DUDE.

ALTERNATIVELY, HELEN'S MAMA IS THE GODDESS NEMESIS, WHO TAKES THE LOGICAL DECISION OF TURNING INTO A FUCKING GOOSE WHEN ZEUS PURSUES HER AS A SWAN.

EITHER WAY WE SUSPECT FOWL PLAY.

HERA PLAYS THE GAME OF THRONES

WHEN HEPHAESTUS IS BORN, HE'S KIND OF UGLY LOOKING, SO HERA DECIDES THE BEST THING TO DO WITH AN UGLY SON IS TO JUST FUCKING THROW HIM OFF MOUNT OLYMPUS.

THIS DOESN'T MAKE HIM ANY LESS UGLY, BUT NOW HE'S LIMPY TOO. BABY HEPHAESTUS IS RAISED BY SOME SEA NYMPHS AND BECOMES SERIOUSLY FUCKING GOOD AT ARTS AND CRAFTS, SPECIFICALLY METAL-WORK (WHICH IS CLEARLY DONE BEST UNDER THE SEA. DON'T QUESTION THE LOGIC HERE).

WHEN HEPHAESTUS GROWS UP HE RETURNS TO OLYMPUS AND GIVES THE OTHER GODS SOME FANCY-ASS THRONES. HERA'S IS EXTRA PRETTY, SO SHE GETS EXCITED AND SITS IN IT IMMEDIATELY.
WRONG MOVE MOTHERFUCKER. THE THRONE IS BOOBY TRAPPED AND CHAINS HER INTO IT. EVERYONE LAUGHS BUT THEN IT'S FUCKING AWKWARD BECAUSE HERA IS NOT THE BEST GODDESS TO PISS OFF.

DIONYSUS' CUNNING PLAN TO RESOLVE THE TENSION IS TO GET HEPHAESTUS SHIT-FACED DRUNK AND PERSUADE HIM TO RELEASE HER. HE DOES SO, AND EVERYONE'S SO GOSH DARN IMPRESSED AT THIS THRONE BOOBY TRAP THING THAT HEPHAESTUS BECOMES THE GOD OF METAL WORK.

DEMETER GETS DOWN AND DIRTY

IT'S THE WEDDING OF CADMUS (THE THEBES GUY) AND HARMONIA. EVERYONE FUCKING LOVES A WEDDING, ESPECIALLY THE GODS, WHO'VE ALL SHOWN UP FOR THE EVENT. THIS USUALLY DOESN'T END WELL, BUT THEY PROVIDE THE FOOD SO NO ONE GIVES A FUCK.

ANYWAY, DURING THE FESTIVITIES, DEMETER DRAGS A YOUNG MORTAL HOTTIE (IASION) AWAY FROM THE PARTY. DEMETER IS SO DAMN INTO NATURE AND FIELDS AND ALL THAT FUCKERY THAT SHE BANGS IASION THEN AND THERE IN A FIELD. CLASSY.

THE PAIR CREEP BACK TO THE WEDDING PARTY, BUT THEY AREN'T EXACTLY SUBTLE. DEMETER'S BUTT IS COVERED IN MUD FROM THE FIELD, SO ZEUS KNOWS WHAT' GONE DOWN. SOMEWHAT HYPOCRITICALLY, ZEUS IS SUPER MAD AT DEMETER FOR FUCKING THIS MORTAL, SO HE ZAPS THE FUCK OUT OF IASION WITH HIS MOTHERFUCKING LIGHTNING.

DEMETER ENDS UP HAVING A SON (OR SEVERAL) BY IASION - PLOUTOS, THE GOD OF WEALTH, SO EVERYBODY WINS (EXCEPT IASION...)

SISTERS AGAINST INCEST

DANAUS HAS FIFTY FUCKING DAUGHTERS; WHAT SOME, INCLUDING HIS WIFE, WOULD CONSIDER TOO DAMN MANY. DANAUS' BROTHER AEGYPTUS HAS FIFTY SONS. ALSO FAR TOO MANY BUT SO FUCKING CONVENIENT.

AEGYPTUS WANTS ALL OF HIS SONS TO MARRY THEIR COUSINS, BECAUSE FINDING SOMEONE NOT RELATED TO YOU TO MARRY IS SO FUCKING HARD. DANAUS DOESN'T WANT HIS DAUGHTERS TO MARRY THEIR COUSINS, BECAUSE THAT'S FUCKING WEIRD. HE AND HIS DAUGHTERS RUN AWAY AS FAST AS POSSIBLE.

EVENTUALLY AEGYPTUS AND HIS SONS CATCH UP WITH THEM, AND DANAUS RELUCTANTLY AGREES TO THIS INCEST FUCKERY. BUT DADDY ISN'T GOING TO LET THIS HAPPEN, SO HE TELLS HIS GIRLS TO MURDER THE FUCK OUT OF THEIR HUSBANDS ON THEIR WEDDING NIGHTS.

THE DAUGHTERS DO THIS AND ALL MURDER THEIR HUSBANDS BECAUSE VIOLENCE IS ALWAYS THE FUCKING ANSWER. THE ONLY EXCEPTION IS HYPERMNESTRA, WHO'S JUST TOO FUCKING GOOD FOR A BIT OF CASUAL BEDSIDE MURDER.

DANAUS THEN HAS THE PROBLEM OF ACTUALLY FINDING PROPER HUSBANDS FOR HIS MURDER-DAUGHTERS, SO INSTEAD OF ANY MARRYING FOR LOVE DISNEY CRAP HE HAS A RUNNING RACE AND LET THE VARIOUS SUITORS PICK A DAUGHTER IN THE ORDER THEY FINISH. CLEVER.

SOME TIME LATER WHEN THE GIRLS DIE, THEY GET PUNISHED IN TARTARUS FOR THE MURDERING INCIDENT. THE MOST CREATIVE THING THE FOLKS DOWNSTAIRS CAN COME UP WITH IS TO HAVE THE DAUGHTERS FETCH WATER IN SOME SHITTY HOLE-FILLED JARS. WELL AT LEAST IT ISN'T THE FIERY WHEEL OF DEATH.

PERSEUS

ACRISIUS, THE KING OF ARGOS, DOESN'T HAVE ANY SONS. THIS IS A BIG FUCKING PROBLEM FOR HIM, SO HE GOES TO DELPHI TO ASK ABOUT HOW HE COULD GET AN HEIR. AS USUAL, THE ORACLE COMPLETELY AVOIDS THE FUCKING QUESTION, AND JUST TOLD HIM THAT HIS GRANDSON WOULD KILL HIM. NATURALLY ACRISIUS FREAKED THE FUCK OUT AND LOCKED HIS DAUGHTER DANAE UP IN SHINY BRONZE PRISON CELL.

ZEUS LOVES FORBIDDEN PRINCESS LADIES, SO HE TURNS INTO A CLOUD OF GOLD (BECAUSE HE'S ZEUS AND HE FUCKING CAN) AND SLEEPS WITH DANAE. NINE MONTHS DOWN THE LINE DANAE GIVES BIRTH TO A CUTE BABY BOY, PERSEUS. ACRISIUS, SINCE HE IS A COMPLETE DICK, SERIOUSLY OVER-REACTS AND THROWS DANAE AND STINKY BABY PERSEUS IN A WOODEN BOX AND CHUCKS IT IN THE FUCKING SEA.

UNUSUALLY, ZEUS ACTUALLY SEEMS TO GIVE A SHIT ABOUT DANAE AND HIS FUCKING SON, SO HE MAKES SURE THEY WASH UP SAFELY ON SOME SHITTY ISLAND. SOME FISHERMAN (DICTYS) HELPS BRING PERSEUS UP AND TRAIN HIM IN MANLY SHIT. THEN DICTYS' ASSHOLE BROTHER POLYDECTES WANTS TO MARRY DANAE, BUT PERSEUS ISN'T HAVING ANY OF THAT SHIT. POLYDECTES KNOWS THAT PERSEUS IS COCK-BLOCKING HIM, SO TO GET HIM TO FUCK OFF HE HAS SOME SHITTY PARTY WHERE EVERYONE HAD TO GIVE HIM A FUCKING HORSE. HE KNOWS THAT PERSEUS HAS NO HORSES TO GIVE, AND GOOD-GUY PERSEUS FEELS GUILTY ABOUT THIS, SO TELLS POLYDECTES HE'LL GET HIM WHATEVER HE FUCKING WANTS. POLYDECTES ASKS FOR THE HEAD OF THE GORGON MEDUSA. HE'S A GREEDY ASSHOLE.

PERSEUS THEN SCAMPERS OFF ON HIS QUEST, FIRST ASKING THE GRAEAE (THE CREEPY OLD LADIES WHO SHARE ONE TOOTH AND EYE BETWEEN THEM) TO TELL HIM WHERE HE COULD FIND THE HESPERIDES (STUPID-ASS PERSEUS, THEIR NAME FUCKING MEANS PEOPLE WHO LIVE IN THE WEST!). THE HESPERIDES AND

SOME OF THE GODS GIVE PERSEUS A SHIT TONNE OF FLASHY GIFTS (FASHIONABLE BACKPACK, SWORD, HADES' HAT, HERMES' HAT. WHO THE FUCK WEARS TWO HATS AT A TIME?)

PERSEUS THEN SHOWS UP AT MEDUSA'S HOME AND FUCKING KILLS HER WITH THE SNEAKY SHIELD-REFLECTION TRICK. COMPLETE ASSHOLERY RIGHT THERE, IT'S NOT LIKE IT WAS HER FAULT FOR GETTING RAPED IN A TEMPLE THEN CURSED BY ATHENA.

WHILE PERSEUS IS GOING AFTER MEDUSA, CASSIOPEIA, QUEEN OF ETHIOPIA (MYTHICAL ETHIOPIA THAT IS, NOWHERE NEAR FUCKING AFRICA) HAS JUST MADE THE STUPID-ASS MOVE OF SAYING HER DAUGHTER ANDROMEDA IS HOTTER THAN ALL OF THE FUCKING SEA-NYMPHS. THIS PISSES POSEIDON OFF BECAUSE HE LOVES HIS FUCKING SEA-NYMPHS, SO HE SENDS A HUGE FUCKING SEA-MONSTER TO FUCK SHIT UP.

OF COURSE, THE ONLY WAY TO STOP THE SEA-MONSTER EATING EVERYTHING IS TO SACRIFICE PRINCESS ANDROMEDA. HER ASSHOLE FATHER CEPHEUS JUMPS AT THE OPPORTUNITY TO TIE HIS NAKED, SCREAMING DAUGHTER TO A ROCK AND WAIT FOR THE SEA-MONSTER TO EAT HER. PERSEUS HAS FINISHED BEATING UP MEDUSA BY NOW, AND ON HIS WAY HOME. HE OVERHEARS ABOUT SOME HOT NAKED LADY BEING CHAINED TO A ROCK, AND FEELS IT'S HIS HEROIC DUTY TO MEDDLE. HE THEN FUCKING TURNS THE SEA-MONSTER TO STONE WITH MEDUSA'S FUCKING DECAPITATED HEAD (HANDILY STORED IN HIS FASHIONABLE BACKPACK). HAVING SAVED THE CITY AND THE GIRL, HE MARRIES ANDROMEDA AND EVERYTHING IS FUCKING GREAT.

BUT WHAT ABOUT THE FUCKING PROPHECY ABOUT PERSEUS KILLING HIS GRANDAD ACRISIUS? SOME TIME LATER, PERSEUS IS SERIOUSLY FUCKING EXCITED BECAUSE HE'S JUST INVENTED THE QUOIT (SERIOUSLY DANGEROUS FUCKING DEATH-FRISBEE). HE GIVES A DEMONSTRATION OF HIS NEW TOY AT SOME FUCKING FESTIVAL, AND GUESS WHO HE ACCIDENTALLY HITS AND KILLS? FUCKING GRANDAD.

FINALLY PERSEUS GETS EXILED FOR HIS FUCKING DEATH-FRISBEE, BUT ALL IS FINE BECAUSE HE FUCKS OFF AND FOUNDS MYCENAE.

ACHILLES IS ONE HOT LADY

THIS ACHILLES BITCH GOT A WHOLE FUCKING EPIC ABOUT HIS MOPING AT TROY, BUT WHAT THE FUCK WAS HE DOING BEFORE THAT? HIS STORY STARTS WHEN HE'S AN ANGRY BUT HEROIC BABY, AND HIS IRRESPONSIBLE MOTHER THETIS FUCKING DIPS HIM IN THE RIVER STYX TO MAKE HIM INVULNERABLE (EXCEPT ONE SHITTY LITTLE PART OF HIS ANKLE) - ALTERNATIVELY SHE COVERS HIM IN AMBROSIA AND SETS HER BABY ON FUCKING FIRE; HIS DAD PELEUS SEES THIS AND FREAKS THE FUCK OUT, SO THE RITUAL IS LEFT INCOMPLETE.

ACHILLES GROWS UP AND GETS TRAINED IN HIPPY HEALING SHIT BY THIS CENTAUR FUCKER CHIRON, AND IN WAR BY THE AWESOMELY NAMED FUCKER PHOENIX. HE'S A FUCKING FABULOUSLY KIDDO AND KILLS LIONS AND SHIT WHEN HE'S SIX YEARS OLD. WHEN HE TURNS NINE, MUMMY THETIS HEARS THE PROPHECY THAT IF HE GOES TO TROY HE'LL NEVER FUCKING COME BACK. TO AVOID THIS, SHE HIDES HIM ON THE ISLAND OF SKYROS.

RATHER THAN JUST HIDING IN THE WOODS OR SOME SHIT, THETIS HAS KID-ACHILLES DRESSED UP AS A GIRL AND HE GROWS UP WITH THE KING OF SKYROS' DAUGHTERS. CLEARLY SOME SHIT GOES DOWN AS ONE OF THE DAUGHTERS, DEIDAMEA, GIVES BIRTH TO HIS SON, THE COMPLETE FUCKING ASSHOLE SHIT-FUCKER DOUCHEBAG CALLED NEOPTOLEMUS (ALSO KNOWN AS PYRRHUS BECAUSE HE'S A FUCKING GINGER).

ACHILLES LOOKS SO DAMN GOOD IN A DRESS THAT HE GETS AWAY WITH THIS FOR YEARS, UNTIL ONE DAY FUCKING ODYSSEUS ROCKS UP, BECAUSE HE'S LOOKING FOR FUCKERS TO PARTY AT TROY. ODYSSEUS CARELESSLY LEAVES SOME WEAPONS LYING AROUND THEN PRETENDS EVERYONE IS UNDER ATTACK. ACHILLES SNAPS INTO HERO-MODE, RIPPING OFF HIS DRESS FUCKING DRAMATICALLY AND GRABBING THE WEAPONS, GIVING UP WITH THE DUMB-SHIT HIDING.

ACHILLES GOES TO TROY, FUCKS SHIT UP AND KILLS BASICALLY FUCKING EVERYONE (EXCEPT PATROCLUS, WHO HE WAS CLEARLY JUST FUCKING), AND LATER IS KILLED BY THAT LOSER PARIS, USING A FUCKING BOW (WHAT A PUSSY) AND PROBABLY WITH APOLLO'S HELP (BECAUSE REALLY PARIS IS ONLY GOOD AT LOOKING HOT AND FUCKING SHIT UP).

HERMES

HERMES IS SUCH A GOSH DARN CUTE LITTLE BABY. ON THE DAY HE'S FUCKING BORN, HIS SOMEWHAT IRRESPONSIBLE MOTHER MAIA LETS HIM GO ON AN ADVENTURE. HE TAKES WITH HIM SOME SHITTY TORTOISE HE FOUND, AS A CUTE PET. EXCEPT HE GETS BORED WITH THE LITTLE SHIT AND RIPS IT OUT OF ITS SHELL, PERFECT FOR MAKING A HANDY LYRE. SADISTIC LITTLE FUCK.

HERMES' AIM IS TO STEAL HIS BROTHER APOLLO'S HERD OF CATTLE; EITHER BECAUSE HE WANTS TO BE A HERDSMAN, OR BECAUSE HE'S JUST FUCKING HUNGRY. HE SOON GETS TO THE CATTLE, AND HIS CUNNING PLAN INVOLVES GIVING THEM SOME SNAZZY BOOTS, SO THEY CAN'T BE TRACKED. HE ALSO PUTS HIS OWN SANDALS ON BACKWARDS TO MAKE THINGS CONFUSING. PRETTY FUCKING SNEAKY FOR A NEWBORN BABY.

HERMES CASUALLY LEADS THOSE BOVINE FUCKERS AWAY, THINKING BACKWARDS FOOTPRINTS MEAN THEY CAN'T BE TRACKED. CUNNING. HERMES HIDES THE CATTLE, GOES BACK TO HIS SHITTY CAVE AND HIDES IN HIS LITTLE CRADLE.

APOLLO IS THE GOD OF FUCKING PROPHECY SO IT DOESN'T TAKE HIM LONG TO FIND OUT WHAT FUCKERY HAS GONE DOWN. HE SHOWS UP AT HERMES' CAVE REALLY MAD, BUT CUTE ICKLE HERMES IS JUST SLEEPING ADORABLY. APOLLO DOESN'T GIVE A SHIT, GRABS HIS BABY BROTHER AND GOES TO COMPLAIN TO DADDY ZEUS.

HERMES GIVES ZEUS SOME SHITTY EXCUSES, BUT EVENTUALLY CONFESSES. ZEUS JUST FINDS ALL THIS SHIT SO FUCKING HILARIOUS HE LETS HIM OFF, AS LONG AS THE BROTHERS GET ALONG.

SO HERMES GIVES APOLLO THE SHITTY LYRE HE MADE FROM HIS TORTOISE BUDDY, AND APOLLO GIVES HERMES SOME FLASHY STICK FOR HERDING CATTLE WITH, AND THEY BECOME BEST

BUDDIES. FINALLY ZEUS MAKES HERMES HIS MESSENGER, TO KEEP THE LITTLE FUCKER OUT OF MISCHIEF.

PARIS DEALS WITH AN EX

REMEMBER HOW PARIS, BEFORE HE GOT INTO ALL THAT BEAUTY CONTEST SHIT AND FUCKED OFF WITH HELEN, LIVED ON A MOUNTAIN AND WAS ALL RUSTIC AND SHIT? BACK WHEN HE HAD THE FARM-BOY THING GOING, HE WAS MARRIED TO SOME NYMPH FUCKER OENONE, THEY EVEN HAD A CHILD TOGETHER.

PARIS DOESN'T GIVE A FUCK ABOUT THIS WHEN HE GETS OFFERED THE SEXIEST LADY IN THE WORLD BY APHRODITE, SO HE JUST FUCKS OFF ON A WOMAN-STEALING MISSION, MEGA-DUMPING OENONE. SHE'S FUCKING PISSED AT HIM, AND ONE VERSION HAS HER EVEN SEND HER SON TO GO AND GUIDE THE GREEKS TOWARDS TROY TO FUCK SHIT UP. SHE'S ALSO ONE OF THE MANY FUCKERS TO PROPHESY TROY'S DESTRUCTION.

SOME YEARS LATER, THE TROJAN WAR IS GETTING FUCKING BORING - HECTOR, ACHILLES AND BIG AJAX ARE DEAD AND EVERYONE JUST WANTS THIS SHIT TO END. THAT STINKY FUCKER PHILOCTETES, BECAUSE HE HAD THE SPECIAL HERACLES BOW, PRIVILEGED FUCKER, WENT AND FUCKING WOUNDED PARIS.

PARIS HAS THIS SHITTY INJURY THAT'S GOING ICKY, AND THE ONLY FUCKER WITH THE MAGIC/HERBAL SKILL TO SAVE HIM? HIS FUCKING EX, OENONE. PARIS CRAWLS ALL THE WAY UP HER MOUNTAIN TO BEG HER TO SAVE HIM, BUT SHE TELLS HIM TO FUCK OFF. REASONABLE. PARIS DIES MISERABLY, BUT FINALLY OENONE IS A BIT UPSET ABOUT THIS, SO THROWS HERSELF ONTO HIS FUNERAL PYRE. WE LOVE A HAPPY ENDING.

PAN FUCKS EVERYTHING

ALL THE GREEK GODS SLEEP AROUND ONE HELL OF A LOT. HERMES ONCE GOT A GIRL PREGNANT WITH A HALF GOD, HALF GOAT MONSTER GOD THING, LATER KNOWN AS PAN. PAN HAD A PRETTY FUCKED UP LIFE. WHEN HIS MOTHER LOOKED AT HER NEW BABY, HE WAS SO FUCKING HIDEOUS THAT SHE SCREAMED AND RAN AWAY. AS A RESULT, PAN ISN'T VERY GOOD WITH WOMEN.

PAN IS THE GOD OF NATURE, SO HE SPENDS MOST OF HIS TIME SLEEPING AND PLAYING WITH SHEEP AND BEES. AND NYMPHS. LOTS OF NYMPHS. PAN FUCKS ALL THE NYMPHS. LITERALLY. HE COLLECTS THEM.

ONCE HE TRIES TO RAPE A NYMPH CALLED PITYS, WHO TURNS INTO A TREE, BECAUSE THAT'S WHAT NYMPHS DO WHEN THEY GET SCARED. IT'S LIKE HEDGEHOGS ROLLING UP INTO BALLS, OR POSSUMS PRETENDING TO BE DEAD, ONLY IT'S KIND OF PERMANENT, WHICH DEFEATS THE FUCKING POINT. THEN HE TRIES TO RAPE SYRINX, WHO.... YES, THAT'S RIGHT. TURNS INTO A FUCKING PLANT. SHE RUNS AWAY TO THE RIVER AND TURNS INTO A REED, AT WHICH POINT PAN GETS CONFUSED AND HASN'T A FUCKING CLUE WHICH REEDS ARE REEDS AND WHICH ARE NYMPHS, SO HE CUTS THEM ALL DOWN AND MAKES PIPES OUT OF THEM. CREEPY BASTARD.

AT ONE POINT HE COVERS HIMSELF IN WOOL AND PRETENDS TO BE A SHEEP TO SEDUCE SELENE. PRESUMABLY HE'S A REALLY FUCKING SEXY SHEEP. EITHER THAT OR SELENE HAS SOME FUCKED UP KINKS.

ACHILLES GETS HEARTBROKEN (AGAIN)

PENTHESILEA IS THE UTTERLY BADASS BETTER-THAN-YOU AMAZON QUEEN. WHILE ALL THAT TROY SHIT IS GOING DOWN, SHE FUCKS UP AND KILLS HER SISTER. OOPS. SHE FEELS SO FUCKING GUILTY SHE WANTS TO GO OFF AND DIE A HEROIC DEATH ASAP.

SHE JOINS THE TROJAN SIDE WITH SOME OF HER AMAZON CROWD. PROBABLY A BAD CALL BECAUSE TROY'S CHIEF GREEK-WHACKER HECTOR HAS JUST BEEN KILLED. THE AMAZONS KILL A SHIT TONNE OF GREEK ASSHOLES, BUT THEN AJAX (THE BIG ONE) ROCKS UP.

PENTHESILEA IS ALL FOR FIGHTING HIM, BUT HE JUST FUCKING LAUGHS AT HER FOR BEING A LADY, THE SHITMONKEY. THEY HAVE A BIT OF A FIGHT BUT THEN ACHILLES SHOWS UP AND JUST FUCKING KILLS PENTHESILEA WITH ONE MOVE.

ONLY AFTER ACHILLES HAS KILLED HER HE SUDDENLY SEES HOW GOSH FUCKING DARN HOT SHE WAS, AND SO FUCKING BRAVE AND ALL THAT SHIT. HE'S COMPLETELY IN LOVE WITH HER, AND IS HELLA UPSET. ACHILLES IS VERY GOOD AT UPSET. HE EVEN BURIES HER HIMSELF. NICE GUY ACHILLES.

FINALLY SOME ASSHAT THERSITES STARTS CALLING ACHILLES A PUSSY FOR BEING A NICE FUCKING GUY. SO ACHILLES BASHES THAT FUCKER'S BRAINS IN WITH ONE HIT.

DO NOT FUCK WITH ACHILLES ~~(UNLESS YOU HAVE THAT SILLY HERACLES BOW)~~.

ARION

ARION IS A MUSICAL FUCKER FROM THE ISLE OF LESBOS; MAKING HIM A MUSICAL LESBIAN. ONE TIME THIS FUCKER IS SAILING BACK FROM SOME SHIT GREECE'S GOT TALENT MUSIC COMPETITION CRAP, DESPITE SOME ORACLE SAYING HE SHOULDN'T FUCKING SAIL ANYWHERE.

BUT HE FUCKS UP AND GETS KIDNAPPED BY PIRATES, WHO WANT TO STEAL ALL THE SHINY CRAP HE'S WON. THEY EFFECTIVELY MAKE HIM WALK THE FUCKING PLANK, BUT HE BUYS SOME TIME BY PLAYING HIS FUCKING CITHARA AND SINGING ABOUT HOW AWESOME APOLLO IS.

AT THE END OF THE SONG, ARION JUMPS INTO THE SEA, ALL DRESSED UP IN HIS SILLY MUSIC CLOTHES. HELPFULLY, HE'S THE SON OF POSEIDON AND SOME SEA NYMPH, SO NATURALLY A DOLPHIN TURNS UP AND GIVES HIM A FREE RIDE TO LAND. TOO FUCKING CONVENIENT. WHEN HE REACHES LAND HE FUCKS UP AND THE DOLPHIN ENDS UP DEAD, SO THERE'S A SAD LITTLE FUNERAL FOR THE DOLPHIN.

BUT THEN THE PIRATES SHOW UP, SO ARION PUTS THE WORD ABOUT THAT HE DROWNED, AND THAT THE DOLPHIN'S GRAVE IS HIS. WHEN THE PIRATES GO TO LOOK AT IT AND LAUGH, ARION JUST JUMPS OUT AND THEY FREAK THE FUCK OUT. THEN ARION'S TYRANT BUDDY PERIANDER HAS THEM ALL EXECUTED.

FINALLY APOLLO PUTS ARION AND HIS DOLPHIN IN THE STARS BECAUSE WHY THE FUCK NOT.

ATHENA GETS DIRTY

GENERALLY SPEAKING, ATHENA AND HEPHAESTUS HAVE A FUCKING CASUAL CO-WORKER RELATIONSHIP (BECAUSE THEY'RE BOTH SERIOUSLY INTO FUCKING ARTS AND CRAFTS).

THEN ONE TIME ATHENA SHOWS UPTO MAKE WEAPONS AT HEPHAESTUS', BUT HEPHAESTUS HAS BEEN LEFT ALONE BY APHRODITE (AGAIN) AND PROBABLY HAD ONE NECTAR TOO MANY, SO IS GRUMPY AND HORNY.

SO HE RUNS AFTER HIS ARTS AND CRAFTS BUDDY AND TRIES TO FUCKING RAPE HER. WHAT A GREAT BIG BAG OF DICKS. FORTUNATELY, HEPHAESTUS IS SOMEWHAT LIMPY SO HE TAKES AGES TO CATCH HER. WHEN HE DOES SHE PUSHES HIM AWAY LIKE THE BADASS MOTHERFUCKER SHE IS, AND HEPHAESTUS JUST CUMS ALL OVER HER LEG.

ATHENA WIPED THAT SHIT OFF WITH SOME WOOL AND FUCKED OFF, LETTING THE CUM-STAINED WOOL FALL TO THE EARTH. THEN SHIT GETS WEIRD. THE EARTH GETS PREGNANT AND PRODUCES A BABY, ERICHTHONIUS. THE EARTH, GAIA, HAS TOO MANY FUCKING CHILDREN ALREADY AND DUMPS THE BABY WITH ATHENA.

ATHENA DOESN'T UNDERSTAND THIS WHOLE MOTHERHOOD FUCKERY SO SHE JUST DUMPS THE BABY IN A BOX AND LEAVES IT ON THE ACROPOLIS IN ATHENS. MORE GREAT PARENTING TIPS RIGHT HERE.

SHE TELLS THE PRIESTESSES THERE NOT TO OPEN THE FUCKING BOX, BUT OF COURSE THEY DO. LONG STORY SHORT, ERECHTHONIUS BECOMES KING OF FUCKING ATHENS, AND MAY OR MAY NOT HAVE ALSO BEEN A SNAKE WITH A HUMAN HEAD.

WHEN SKINNY-DIPPING GOES WRONG

HERMAPHRODITUS IS THE CREATIVELY NAMED SON OF APHRODITE AND HERMES (YES SHE FUCKING GETS AROUND). GIVEN WHO HIS MUM IS, HE IS OF COURSE SUPER FUCKING HOT.

SALMACIS IS A REALLY FUCKING LAZY NYMPH. ALL SHE FUCKING DOES IS SIT IN HER POND AND DO HER FUCKING HAIR. THE ONE TIME SHE GETS OUT OF HER FUCKING POND SHE BUMPS INTO HERMAPHRODITUS, WHO'S SO DAMN HOT SHE ASKS TO MARRY HIM THEN AND THERE (WHAT THE FUCK GIRL, YOU CAN'T JUST MARRY SOMEONE YOU'VE JUST MET). HERMAPHRODITUS TELLS HER TO FUCK OFF BECAUSE SHE'S CREEPY.

HERMAPHRODITUS GOES FOR A BATH IN SALMACIS' POND, SO SHE HIDES BEHIND A TREE AND WATCHES HIM GET NAKED. CREEP. EVENTUALLY IT'S ALL TOO MUCH AND SHE JUMPS INTO THE POND AFTER HIM TO GET FREAKY IN THE WATER.

HERMAPHRODITUS TRIES TO FIGHT HER OFF, BUT SHE CLINGS ON TO HIM LIKE A HORNY LIMPET. EVENTUALLY SHE PRAYS FOR THEM TO NEVER BE PARTED, WHICH IN HINDSIGHT WAS A FUCKING STUPID IDEA.

INSTEAD OF MAKING HERMAPHRODITUS ACTUALLY LIKE HER, THE GODS JUST MUSHED THEIR BODIES TOGETHER SO THEY BECAME ONE PERSON, WITH GREAT TITS AND A MASSIVE DICK. PERFECT.

MORE CHILD-EATING

PROCNE AND TEREUS ARE MARRIED. HOW FUCKING CUTE. BUT PROCNE'S SISTER PHILOMELA IS HOTTER THAN HER, AND TEREUS TOTALLY WANTS TO TAP THAT.

HE PRETENDS THAT HIS WIFE IS FUCKING DEAD SO HE CAN FUCK HER SISTER. WHAT A COMPLETE ASSHOLE. HE EVEN HAS PROCNE'S TONGUE CUT OUT AND STICKS HER WITH THE SLAVES SO NOBODY CAN EVER THINK SHE'S ALIVE. OF COURSE HE CAN'T JUST FUCKING KILL HER, THAT WOULD BE FAR TOO EASY.

BUT PROCNE WRITES HER SISTER A MESSAGE ON A FUCKING TAPESTRY TO SAY THAT SHE IS VERY MUCH ALIVE AND FUCKING HATES HER HUSBAND. EVERYONE HATES TEREUS. ESPECIALLY HIS BROTHER WHO HE THEN KILLS BECAUSE OF SOME PROPHECY SHIT.

SO THE LADIES PLOT REVENGE IN THE MOST OBVIOUS FUCKING WAY: CHILD-KILLING AND CANNIBALISM. PROCNE GRABS HER OWN SON, KILLS HIM AND BOILS HIM UP FOR DADDY'S DINNER. YUM.

HE SOON REALISES WHAT FUCKERY HAS HAPPENED WHEN THE SISTERS SHOW UP WITH HIS SON'S SEVERED HEAD AND HE RUNS AFTER THEM WITH A FUCKING AXE. BUT BY NOW THE GODS ARE FUCKING BORED OF THIS SHIT SO THEY TURN ALL THREE FUCKERS INTO BIRDS; PROCNE INTO A SWALLOW, PHILOMELA A NIGHTINGALE AND TEREUS A FUCKING HOOPOE. CAW CAW MOTHERFUCKERS.

LETO

SO LETO IS A HOT TITAN LADY AND ZEUS IS HORNY. MOST STORIES FUCKING START LIKE THIS, ALL RIGHT? OF COURSE, HERA HATES ANY BITCH THAT ZEUS FUCKS, SO WHILE LETO IS PREGNANT WITH ZEUS' KIDS SHE CURSES HER SO NO COUNTRY WILL LET HER STOP AND GIVE BIRTH. WHAT A FUCKING DICK MOVE. FOR GOOD MEASURE HERA ALSO SENDS A FUCKING HUGE-ASS SNAKE TO CHASE PREGNANT LETO. THIS IS SOME SERIOUS OVER-REACTING HERE.

THE ONLY PLACE LETO CAN FIND TO STOP RUNNING AND GIVE BIRTH IS THE ISLAND OF DELOS. DELOS USED TO JUST FLOAT AROUND IN THE SEA, WHICH WAS PRETTY FUCKING USELESS. LETO MAKES A DEAL WITH THE ISLAND TO STOP FLOATING AND BE AN ACTUAL ISLAND AND IN RETURN HER SON WILL MAKE IT THE BEST FUCKING ISLAND OUT THERE.

SO LETO POPS OUT A BABY. IT'S THE GODDESS ARTEMIS, HOW FUCKING CUTE. BABY ARTEMIS THEN HELPS LETO DELIVER HER TWIN BROTHER APOLLO, BECAUSE SHE WAS A FUCKING RESOURCEFUL BABY.

SOMETIME LATER A NASTY-ASS GIANT CALLED TITYOS ~~EHE TITTIES~~ TRIES TO KIDNAP AND RAPE LETO. BUT APOLLO IS HAVING NONE OF THIS SHIT AND KILLS THE FUCK OUT OF THE GIANT. HE ALSO KILLS THE NASTY-ASS SNAKE THAT CHASED HIS MAMA AROUND. BASICALLY APOLLO IS GREAT AT KILLING SHIT, FUCKING SHIT AND WRITING POETRY ABOUT THE TWO.

SISYPHUS IS A COMPLETE ASSHOLE

SISYPHUS IS THE MOTHERFUCKER WITH THE SUPER CREATIVE "ROLL THE STONE UP THE HILL AND WATCH IT FALL DOWN FOR FUCKING EVER" PUNISHMENT IN THE UNDERWORLD. THAT MUST FUCKING SUCK, BUT HE SURE AS SHIT DESERVES IT, BECAUSE HE MANAGES QUITE EFFECTIVELY TO MAKE EVERYONE HATE HIM.

FIRSTLY, HE'S A DICK TO GUESTS AND KILLS PEOPLE IN HIS OWN FUCKING HOME. THAT'S NOT XENIA, MOTHERFUCKER.

ONE TIME HE HAPPENS TO SEE ZEUS KIDNAPPING YET ANOTHER NYMPH. HE THEN TELLS HER ANGRY FATHER WHERE ZEUS HAS TAKEN HER, SERIOUSLY PISSING THE BIG GUY OFF.

SO ZEUS ORDERS DEATH (THANATOS) TO COME AND CHAIN SISYPHUS UP IN TARTARUS (MEANEST NASTIEST CORNER OF THE UNDERWORLD). DEATH SHOWS UP, EXCITED TO USE HIS NEW FANCY CHAINS. SISYPHUS ASKS HIM IF HE COULD KINDLY DEMONSTRATE HOW THE FUCK ONE USES THESE FANCY CHAINS, SO DEATH CHAINS HIMSELF UP WITH THEM, TO SHOW HOW FUCKING GREAT THEY ARE.

ONCE HE'S NICE AND CHAINED UP, SISYPHUS CHUCKS DEATH IN A CUPBOARD AND CONTINUES BEING A DICK TO PEOPLE. BUT NOW NOBODY IS DYING BECAUSE DEATH IS TIED UP, AND THIS IS NO FUCKING FUN FOR ARES. TONNES OF FUCKERS ARE GETTING CUT TO BITS IN BATTLE AND NOT DYING. IT SUCKS. SO ARES FREES DEATH AND EVENTUALLY SISYPHUS FUCKING DIES.

BEFORE HE DOES SO, HE TELLS HIS WIFE TO LEAVE HIS BODY JUST FUCKING LYING AROUND. WHEN HE GOES TO THE UNDERWORLD HE WHINES TO PERSEPHONE ABOUT NOT HAVING A PROPER FUNERAL AND ISN'T THAT FUCKING SAD. SHE LETS HIM GO BACK TO THE WORLD TO TELL HIS WIFE TO BURY HIM, BUT OF COURSE HE DOESN'T DO THAT, HE JUST DICKS AROUND AS A GHOST FOR A BIT.

FINALLY HERMES COMES AND DRAGS HIM BACK TO THE UNDERWORLD, AND SISYPHUS STARTS HIS ROCK AND ROLL CAREER.

HUNGRY HUNGRY HIPPO

NO SMALL PLASTIC HIPPOS HERE AT ALL. SORRY, MOTHERFUCKERS.

ERYSICHTHON IS SOME BITCHIN' KING OF THESSALY. ONE TIME DEMETER MENTIONS SOME SHIT ABOUT HOW HE SHOULD BUILD A FUCKING BIG DINING ROOM BECAUSE HE NEEDS TO HAVE ALL THE FUCKING FEASTS. SO ERYSICHTHON BUILDS A DINING ROOM. NOT JUST A SMALL SHITTY ONE, A FUCKING MASSIVE ONE. HE HAS ALL THE TREES CUT DOWN, INCLUDING A SUPER SPECIAL GROVE BELONGING TO DEMETER. HE ALSO HACKS A TREE NYMPH TO BITS BECAUSE HE'S A FUCKING TWAT.

DEMETER IS PISSED OFF BECAUSE SHE FUCKING LOVED THOSE TREES. SHE CURSES ERYSICHTHON TO BE PERMANENTLY HUNGRY. THE MORE HE FUCKING EATS THE HUNGRIER HE GETS. ~~WE FEEL LIKE THAT SOMETIMES.~~
HE EATS FUCKING EVERYTHING, EVEN HIS HORSES, MULES AND FAMILY PETS. WHAT A DICK. EVENTUALLY HE RUNS OUT OF MONEY FOR FOOD, BUT THAT'S NO PROBLEM; HE JUST SELLS HIS FUCKING DAUGHTER.

LUCKILY HIS DAUGHTER HAD RAD-ASS SHAPE-SHIFTING POWERS BECAUSE SHE FUCKED POSEIDON A WHILE BACK, SO SHE ESCAPES AND THEN ERYSICHTHON KEEPS RE-SELLING HER AS DIFFERENT ANIMALS FOR MORE FUCKING FOOD MONEY. CLEVER. HE CAN NEVER STOP BEING HUNGRY THOUGH, SO EVENTUALLY HE JUST FUCKING EATS HIMSELF. WHAT THE ACTUAL FUCK.

HECATE

HECATE IS A SERIOUS BAD-ASS MOTHERFUCKER. WHAT ELSE WOULD YOU EXPECT FROM THE GODDESS OF FUCKING MAGIC?

SHE'S THE ONE WHO HELPED DEMETER LOOK FOR PERSEPHONE AFTER THAT KIDNAP BUSINESS, BECAUSE SHE HAD SOME BITCHIN' TORCHES WHICH ARE FUCKING GREAT FOR SEARCHING FOR LOST DAUGHTERS. WHEN THAT FUCKERY ALL SORTED ITSELF OUT, HECATE BECAME BESTIES WITH HADES AND PERSEPHONE AND LANDED A JOB DOING SERIOUS UNDERWORLD BUSINESS.

AS GODDESS OF FUCKING WITCHCRAFT, SHE HAS SOME BADASS FAMILIARS; A POLECAT AND A BLACK DOG. OF COURSE THIS ISN'T JUST ANY OLD DOG, THIS DOG USED TO BE FUCKING HECUBA, QUEEN OF FUCKING TROY.

THE POLECAT USED TO BE SOME WITCH CALLED GALE, WHOM HECATE TURNED INTO A SHITTY WEASEL FOR "INCONTINENCE AND ABNORMAL SEXUAL DESIRES". WHAT THE FUCK.
HECATE IS USUALLY REFERRED TO AS A VIRGIN GODDESS, BECAUSE SHE'S TOO FUCKING GOOD FOR SOME BLOKE.

OH AND SHE'S ASSOCIATED WITH CROSSROADS (THE BEST PLACES FOR ALL YOUR MAGIC AND NECROMANCY FUCKERY), SO SOMETIMES SHE FACES THREE WAYS IN STATUES, SO SHE CAN DEATH-GLARE YOU FUCKERS FROM ALL ANGLES.

ROMAN MYTHOLOGY

[ROME INTENSIFIES]

A LONG TIME AGO IN ALBA LONGA, RHEA SILVIA IS THE SEXY ASS NIECE OF ASSHOLE KING AMULIUS. SHE'S ALSO SUPPOSED TO BE A FUCKING VESTAL VIRGIN, THOUGH THAT DOESN'T STOP MARS KNOCKING HER UP. NINE MONTHS LATER SHE GIVES BIRTH TO TWINS ROMULUS AND REMUS. BEING A COMPLETE FUCKING DICK, AMULIUS HAS RHEA FUCKING DROWNED, AND ALSO THROWS HER NEWBORN SONS IN THE RIVER.

NATURALLY THIS IS FUCKING POINTLESS AS THEY HAVE MAGICAL ABANDONED BABY POWERS, AND EVENTUALLY WASH UP ON THE RIVERBANK. THEN EVERYTHING GETS VERY DISNEY WHEN A MOTHER WOLF NURTURES THEM AS HER OWN. WOLVES AREN'T THE BEST CHILD-MINDERS, SO LUCKILY A SHEPHERD ARRIVES AND ADOPTS THE LIL SHITS. SAID SHITS GROW UP TO BECOME BITCHIN' WARRIORS AND START THIEVING THINGS FROM OTHER THIEVES.

REMUS IS EVENTUALLY CAUGHT AND PUT BEFORE THEIR NOT-SO-GREAT-UNCLE KING AMULIUS. ROMULUS THEN COMES TO RESCUE HIM AND MURDERS EVERY SINGLE FUCKING PERSON THERE. THEIR GRANDFATHER NUMITOR THEN BECOMES KING OF ALBA LONGA, RECOGNISES THEM AS HIS FAMILY, AND EVERYTHING IS GREAT.

UNTIL THE TWINS GET POWER HUNGRY, AND BUILD THEIR OWN CITY, BECAUSE THEY FUCKING CAN. ROMULUS STARTS BUILDING THE WALLS, BUT REMUS JUST DICKS AROUND, JUMPS OVER THE SHITTY WALLS AND LAUGHS AT HIS BROTHER. SO ROMULUS GETS MAD AND FUCKING KILLS THE LITTLE SHIT.

ROME - THE ETERNAL CITY, THE GREATEST CITY, ALL FOUNDED BY A BROTHER-KILLING ASSHOLE, AND ORIGINALLY POPULATED BY THIEVES, EX-SLAVES, MURDERERS, AND RAPISTS (THE ONLY PEOPLE ROMULUS COULD CONVINCE TO VISIT HIS SHITTY LITTLE CITY). FUCK YES ROMAN PRIDE.

ROMANS ARE DICKS

ROMULUS HAS JUST BUILT ROME. HE NEEDS SOME PEOPLE, BUT THE ONLY FUCKERS HE CAN CONVINCE TO JOIN HIM ARE RUNAWAY CRIMINALS, SO NOT MANY WOMEN.

SO THE ROMANS DEVELOP A WOMAN-STEALING PLOT. THEY INVITE THE NEIGHBOURING FUCKERS, THE SABINES, TO SOME SHITTY FESTIVAL THEY'RE HAVING. EVERYONE FUCKING LOVES THE PARTY AND THE CITY, SO DOESN'T GIVE MUCH OF A FUCK WHEN ALL THE ROMAN ASSHOLES GRAB THE WOMEN, WHOM THE SABINES HAVE HELPFULLY TAKEN WITH THEM. THE SABINE MEN RUN OFF, PRESUMABLY BECAUSE THE ROMANS HAVE TAKEN THEIR WOMEN AND WERE ALSO SCARY ASSHOLES.

SOMETIME LATER THE SABINES DECLARE WAR ON THE ROMANS, AND DURING THIS SOME ROMAN BITCH CALLED TARPEIA DECIDES TO BE A FUCKING TRAITOR AND OPEN THE FUCKING GATES. SHE ENDS UP CRUSHED TO DEATH, SO EVERYTHING WORKS OUT FINE (ALSO SHE'S THROWN FROM THIS SPECIAL ROCK THAT'S HELLA USEFUL FOR CHUCKING TRAITORS FROM).

THERE'S ABOUT TO BE THIS FUCKING DRAMATIC BATTLE WHEN SUDDENLY THE WOMEN, NOW ALL HAPPILY MARRIED TO ROMANS, RUN OUT IN THE MIDDLE OF THE FUCKING BATTLE AND WAVE THEIR BABIES IN THE AIR. BECAUSE THAT'S THE FUCKING UNIVERSAL SIGN FOR PEACE.

HOLY FLYING DICK, BATMAN!

A VESTAL VIRGIN, OCRISIA, IS CASUALLY TENDING THE SUPER SACRED FIRE, AS YOU'D FUCKING EXPECT.

THEN A FLYING DICK JUMPS OUT FROM THE FUCKING FIRE. THE GIRL FREAKS THE FUCK OUT, BUT LUCKILY THE QUEEN, TANAQUIL, IS ON HAND TO HELP. SHE GIVES HER SOME SEXY CLOTHES AND LOCKS HER IN THE ROOM WITH THE FLYING DICK, WHAT THE ACTUAL FUCK, TANAQUIL? LONG STORY SHORT OCRISIA GETS PREGNANT.

THE DICK BELONGS TO EITHER VULCAN OR POSSIBLY THE FAMILY LAR (EXTREMELY NEEDY HOUSEHOLD SPIRITS), AND PRESUMABLY HE NEVER FUCKING CALLS BACK. THE CHILD BORN IS SERVIUS TULLIUS, AND BECAUSE HE HAS DIVINE PARENTAGE, HE GETS TO MARRY THE KING'S DAUGHTER, AND BECOMES THE NEXT KING. HE HAS A VAGUELY HAPPY LIFE BEATING THE SHIT OUT OF LOCAL TRIBES AND IS EVENTUALLY MURDERED.

LIVY ALSO HAS A VERSION OF SERVIUS' ORIGIN STORY, BUT IT'S WAY LESS FUN AND ONLY HAS A CHILD RANDOMLY BURSTING INTO FLAME (A COMMON ANCIENT AFFLICTION).

CRAZY OLD LADY BURNS BOOKS

THE SYBIL AT CUMAE, ITALY (THE ONE THAT FUCKER AENEAS MET) WASN'T ALWAYS A FUTURE-SEEING OLD HAG. SHE WAS YOUNG AND HOT ONCE, AND APOLLO WANTED TO FUCK HER. UNLIKE HIS DAD, APOLLO IS LESS RAPEY AND MORE BRIBEY, SO THE SYBIL MANAGES TO TALK HIM INTO GIVING HER FUTURE-SIGHT AND IMMORTALITY. SHE THEN DECIDES SHE DOESN'T WANT TO FUCK HIM, SO APOLLO GETS PISSED AND CURSES HER WITH ETERNAL OLD AGE (BECAUSE HE CAN'T TAKE BACK THE OTHER GIFTS, IT'S IN DA RULEZ AND ALL). EVENTUALLY SHE SHRIVELS AWAY AND LIVES IN A JAR.

ANYWAY, ONE DAY A SYBIL (THERE WERE MORE THAN ONE, IT'S LIKE THE FUCKING GREEN LANTERN OR SOMETHING OK) VISITS THE LAST KING OF ROME (TARQUIN THE PROUD FUCKER) WITH A PILE OF SHITTY LOOKING BOOKS.

SHE DUMPS THE SHITTY LOOKING BOOKS IN FRONT OF THE KING, TELLS HIM THEY'RE SOME SUPER IMPORTANT PROPHECY FUCKERY AND ASKS FOR A STUPID AMOUNT OF MONEY FOR THEM. THE KING LAUGHS AND TELLS HER TO FUCK OFF.

SO SHE FUCKS OFF AND BURNS THREE OF THE BOOKS, QUITE POSSIBLY CACKLING AS SHE DOES SO.

THE OLD LADY COMES BACK AND OFFERS HIM THE SIX REMAINING BOOKS FOR THE SAME STUPID PRICE. HE TELLS HER TO FUCK OFF AGAIN, SO SHE BURNS ANOTHER THREE.

SHE THEN ASKS FOR THE SAME PRICE FOR JUST THREE BOOKS. FINALLY TARQUIN GETS HIS SHIT TOGETHER AND REALISES SPECIAL PROPHECY BOOKS MIGHT BE A FUCKING GREAT IDEA, SO HE BUYS THEM AND STICKS THEM IN A TEMPLE.

WE HAVE NO FUCKING IDEA WHAT THE OLD SYBIL SPENDS THE MONEY ON BUT WE HOPE SHE ENJOYS IT.

TARQUIN CLEARLY DOESN'T READ THE BIT ABOUT HIS DOWNFALL AND THE REPUBLIC THAT REPLACES HIM. THE BOOKS ARE READ WHEN SHIT IS GOING DOWN IN ROME, BECAUSE THERE'S NOTHING MORE REASSURING THAN A WHOLE BOOK OF CRAZY. THE TEMPLE THE BOOKS LIVE IN IS EVENTUALLY BURNT IN THE LATE REPUBLIC (PROBABLY THAT SULLA FUCKER). THIS IS FUCKING AWKWARD SO THE ROMANS GO AROUND COLLECTING SIMILAR PROPHECY SHIT.

FINALLY THEY'RE DESTROYED IN 405AD BY SOME CHRISTIAN FUCKER WHO WANTS TO DESTROY ALL THE EVIL PAGAN FUCKERY. ROME IS FUCKING SACKED FIVE YEARS LATER. COINCIDENCE? WE THINK NOT.

EGYPTIAN MYTHOLOGY

BEGINNINGS: EGYPTIAN STYLE

IN THE BEGINNING THERE'S A FUCK-TONNE OF WATER, MIXED WITH ANOTHER FUCK-TONNE OF DARKNESS. ONE DAY IN THE DARKNESS A BIG SHINY EGG. FROM THIS EGG RA APPEARS, AND SINCE HE'S THE FUCKING SUN GOD THE DARKNESS FUCKS OFF.

HE THEN GOES AROUND MAKING SHIT, THOUGH THAT'S FUCKING INCONVENIENT SO INSTEAD HE JUST NAMES SHIT, LIKE SHU, THE WIND. WHEN HE GIVES SHIT NAMES, THINGS JUST POP INTO EXISTENCE. HE THEN MAKES A FUCK-TONNE MORE GODS, SUCH AS GEB (EARTH) AND NUT (SKY) (THESE TWO FUCKERS ARE A CUTE COUPLE OFC).

NEXT RA WANTS SOME MINIONS SO HE MAKES (NAMES) MANKIND. BECAUSE HUMANS ARE COMPLETE FUCKING IDIOTS AND CAN'T LOOK AFTER THEMSELVES, RA TURNS HIMSELF INTO A MAN AND GOES DOWN TO EARTH TO RULE THEM AS THEIR FIRST PHARAOH. HE RULES FOR THOUSANDS OF YEARS, BUT EVENTUALLY MEN AREN'T FUCKING AFRAID OF HIM ANY MORE BECAUSE HE'S GETTING OLD TOO, AND THEY JUST THINK HE'S KIND OF LAME AND SHITTY.

THIS MAKES RA PRETTY FUCKING MAD. DON'T MAKE RA MAD, HE HAS CLEVER PLANS...

RA'S PUSSY FUCKS SHIT UP

RA WANTS A WAY OF GETTING BACK AT THE HUMANS FOR CALLING HIM MEAN NAMES. SO HE CREATES A METAL-AS-FUCK LIONESS DAUGHTER BY JUST EFFECTIVELY GLARING AT THE HUMANS WITH HIS MAGICAL FUCKING EYE.

HIS DAUGHTER IS SEKHMET, THE CRAZIEST BLOODTHIRSTY LIONESS GODDESS. AS ORDERED SHE GOES AND HUNTS DOWN EVERY SINGLE ONE OF THE FUCKERS WHO OFFENDED RA.

THEN THINGS GET OUT OF HAND AND SEKHMET JUST KEEPS ON WITH HER MURDEROUS RAMPAGE - EVEN HER DADDY RA CAN'T STOP HER FUCKING SHIT UP. BUT AS ALWAYS, RA HAS A PLAN.

RA AND THE OTHER GODS GO AND BUY A SHIT TONNE OF RED DYE, AND USE IT TO COLOUR A BILLION BILLION PINTS OF BEER. THIS MIXER FROM HELL IS THEN LIBERALLY SPREAD IN A LAKE BY THE NEXT TOWN ON SEKHMET'S KILL LIST.

WHEN SHE GETS THERE, SEKHMET IS JUST SO FUCKING BLOOD-CRAZY THAT SHE THINKS IT'S A POOL OF THE OLD O NEG, AND LIES DOWN AND DRINKS FUCKING ALL OF IT. THIS GETS HER COMPLETELY FUCKING WASTED AND SHE PASSES OUT. DRINK RESPONSIBLY, FUCKERS.

SHE EVENTUALLY STAGGERS HOME TO DADDY AND GIVES UP WITH THE WHOLE KILLING SHIT. WHAT A FUCKING INSPIRING STORY.

SIBLINGS FUCK

RA HEARS SOME PROPHECY CRAP ABOUT SOME CHILD OF NUT'S BEING PHAROAH INSTEAD OF HIM. THIS PISSES HIM THE FUCK OFF, SO HE CURSES NUT TO NOT BE ABLE TO HAVE KIDS ON ANY DAY OF THE FUCKING YEAR. WHAT AN ASSHOLE.

THOTH (IBIS GUY) IS TOTALLY IN LOVE WITH NUT (BUT SHE'S INTO GEB. IT'S AN AWKWARD FUCKING LOVE TRIANGLE OK) SO HE WANTS TO HELP HER GET AROUND THE STUPID ASS CURSE. THOTH IS THE GOD OF KNOWLEDGE AND CLEVER SHIT, SO NATURALLY HE HAS A SNEAKY FUCKING PLAN.

HE FINDS THE MOON GOD KHONSU AND MAKES HIM SIT DOWN AND GAMBLE WITH HIM. KHONSU HAS SOME SERIOUS GAMBLING ADDICTION. HE KEEPS PLAYING WITH THOTH EVEN THOUGH THOTH WINS EVERY FUCKING TIME. THE WAGERS GET HIGHER AND HIGHER AND EVENTUALLY KHONSU LOSESFUCKING EVERYTHING TO THOTH. KHONSU IS USING FUCKING LIGHT TO WAGER WITH (SERIOUSLY FUCKING IRRESPONSIBLE), AND SOON HE REALISES HE'S GIVEN THOTH A HUGE FUCKING PILE OF LIGHT, SO HE GIVES UP.

THOTH TURNS THE LIGHT INTO FIVE EXTRA DAYS, AND NUT GOES AND GIVES BIRTH TO OSIRIS, AN ALTERNATE FUCKING HORUS, SETH, ISIS AND NEPHTHYS. FUCKING BABIES EVERYWHERE!

OSIRIS AND ISIS MARRY, SO DO SETH AND NEPHTHYS AND EVERYTHING IS FUCKING INCESTUOUS.

ISIS IS A SNEAKY LITTLE SHIT AND WANTS HER HUSBAND TO BE SUPER POWERFUL. SO NATURALLY SHE USES ALL HER WOMANLY SNEAKINESS TO TRICK RA INTO TELLING HER HIS SUPER FUCKING BADASS SECRET NAME. SHE DOES THIS BY BASICALLY TORTURING HIM WITH SNAKE POISON AND FORCING HIM TO TELL HER. SHE THEN USES THE SUPER POWERFUL SECRET NAME TO MAKE OSIRIS BE PHAROAH, MAKING THE PROPHECY COME TRUE. FUCK YES PROPHECY.

DICK IN A BOX

OSIRIS IS PHAROAH, ISIS IS HIS QUEEN AND EVERYTHING IS FUCKING FABULOUS. THIS MAKES THEIR EVIL BROTHER SETH FUCKING JEALOUS BECAUSE HE'S JUST AN ASSHOLE BASICALLY. SETH GATHERS A SHIT-TONNE OF EVIL CRONIES AND PLANS A HUGE FUCKING PARTY FOR OSIRIS. HE ALSO ORDERS A BIG FLASHY WOODEN BOX MADE EXACTLY TO OSIRIS' MEASUREMENTS.

THE PARTY GETS GOING, AND SOON OSIRIS AND ISIS SHOW UP. ALL THE OTHER GUESTS ARE SETH'S EVIL GANG, SO EVERYTHING IS FUCKING SUSPICIOUS FROM THE START. THEN SETH WHIPS OUT THIS SHINY-ASS BOX, ALL COVERED WITH GOLD AND JEWELS AND SHIT, AND SAYS THAT WHOEVER FITS PERFECTLY IN IT COULD HAVE IT. SETH'S CRONIES ARE ALL COMICALLY FUCKING STUPID SIZES, BECAUSE NOBODY ELSE FITS THIS FUCKING BOX PERFECTLY, EXCEPT OF COURSE OSIRIS. BEFORE OSIRIS HAS TIME TO GET EXCITED ABOUT THE NEW BOX HE WON, SETH JUST NAILS THE FUCKING BOX SHUT.

HE THROWS IT INTO THE NILE, AND SINCE OSIRIS IS AT THIS POINT KIND OF MORTAL HE THEN FUCKING DIES (BECAUSE THE GODS TAKE A MORTAL FORM WHEN ON EARTH, O-FUCKING-KAY). EVENTUALLY THE BOX ENDS UP ON SOME SHITTY BEACH AND ISIS HAS TO GO AND COLLECT IT (IT'S A LONG FUCKING STORY INVOLVING A CHILD DYING OF TERROR AND SOME HAIR BRAIDING).

ISIS GETS THE COFFIN/BOX/BODY THING BACK TO HER SECRET HIDEOUT (BECAUSE SETH IS PHAROAH NOW AND HE'S A COMPLETE ASSHOLE). BUT THEN SETH FINDS IT AND, JUST TO MAKE SURE OSIRIS WOULDN'T GET TO GO TO THE AFTERLIFE OR ANY SHIT LIKE THAT, CUTS THE BODY INTO 14 PIECES AND THREW THEM INTO THE NILE.

ISIS THEN HAS TO GO AROUND SEARCHING FOR THESE PIECES IN SOME FUCKED-UP TREASURE HUNT, AS WELL AS LOOKING

AFTER THEIR BABY SON HORUS. FUCK YES WORKING MOTHERS. EVENTUALLY SHE FINDS ALL THE FUCKING PIECES, EXCEPT OSIRIS' DICK, BECAUSE SOME FISH FUCKING ATE IT. SHE PUTS ALL THE BITS TOGETHER (SHE MAKES HIM A NEW DICK WITH MAGIC, DON'T YOU FUCKERS WORRY), SO FINALLY OSIRIS' SPIRIT IS FREE TO GO AND RULE IN THE FUCKING AFTERLIFE.

SETH AND HORUS FUCK WITH SALAD

THIS SHIT IS FUCKING WEIRD, BRACE YOURSELVES, MOTHERFUCKERS.

HORUS FUCKING HATES SETH, BECAUSE SETH HAS KILLED HIS DADDY OSIRIS AND IS JUST GENERALLY AN ASSHOLE. SETH ALSO HATES HORUS BECAUSE HE JUST HATES EVERYTHING GOOD. THEY HAVE TONNES OF FIGHTS AND SHIT FOR EIGHTY FUCKING YEARS TO GET CONTROL OF EGYPT, UNTIL THIS GETS BORING. ONE DAY SETH THINKS HE'LL SHOW HE'S BETTER THAN HORUS ONCE AND FOR ALL BY FUCKING HIM.

EITHER WAY, SETH MOVES IN TO DO THE DEED, BUT HORUS IS ALL "FUCK NO, UNCLE" AND GRABS HIS DICK OUT OF THE WAY. HE GETS FUCKING CUM ALL OVER HIS HANDS, AND JUST WAVES IT OFF INTO THE NILE. HORUS RUNS AWAY TO SETH'S KITCHEN OR SOME SHIT LIKE THAT THEN JUST FUCKING CUMS ALL OVER SETH'S LETTUCE. SETH'S FAVOURITE FOOD IS LETTUCE, SO NATURALLY HE FALLS INTO THE CUNNING SALAD/SEMEN TRAP AND EATS THE FUCKING LETTUCE.

NOT REALISING HOW FUCKED UP THINGS HAVE GOT, THE OTHER GODS GATHER TOGETHER TO SETTLE THIS STUPID EGYPT ARGUMENT. SETH ARGUES THAT SINCE HE FUCKED HORUS, HE SHOULD HAVE THE THRONE. HORUS AGGRESSIVELY DENIES ANY CANOODLING, AND SAYS TO CALL ON SETH'S CUM AS A WITNESS. THE CUM TAKES TO THE WITNESS BOX AND REPLIES FROM THE NILE. THEN HORUS ASKS ABOUT WHERE HIS CUM HAS GOT TO, AND SINCE IT REPLIES FROM WITHIN SETH, ALL THE OTHER GODS JUMPED TO CONCLUSIONS, AND SAID THAT HORUS WAS THE VICTOR.

SETH STILL WASN'T GIVING UP, SO EVENTUALLY THE THRONE OF EGYPT IS GIVEN TO WHOEVER WINS IN SOME SHITTY BOAT RACE WITH STONE BOATS. HORUS WINS BECAUSE HE FUCKING CHEATS. AND THEY CALL SETH THE EVIL FUCKER!

SCORPIONS ARE FUCKING DANGEROUS

DURING THE GREAT SET/HORUS/OSIRIS MURDER PARTY DEBACLE, ISIS IS HIDING OUT IN SOME SWAMPS. THE CLOSEST THING SHE HAS TO FRIENDS IS A BUNCH OF FUCKING SCORPIONS, WHICH AREN'T EXACTLY CONVERSATIONAL. THEY'RE ALL SHE'S GOT, THOUGH, AND BECAUSE SHE'S LONELY AS FUCK SHE NAMES THEM ALL.

ONE DAY, THEY COME TO A SMALL VILLAGE AND GO LOOKING FOR SOMEWHERE TO SLEEP. AT THE FIRST HOUSE THEY COME TO, THE WOMAN THAT LIVES THERE SEES ISIS AND HER SCORPION BROS, PANICS, AND LOCKS THE FUCKING DOOR. ISIS MOVES ON TO THE NEXT HOUSE, WHERE SHE GETS OFFERED A BED, BUT THE SCORPIONS ARE FUCKING FURIOUS.

THEY SNEAK INTO THE WOMAN'S HOUSE, AND SIX OF THE SEVEN SCORPIONS LEND THEIR POISON TO THE SEVENTH, A SCORPION CALLED TEFEN. TEFEN'S A LITTLE SHIT. HE THEN PROCEEDS TO STING THE WOMAN'S SON IN THE FACE AND ALL THE SCORPIONS FUCK OFF TO BE SMUG ABOUT THEIR CRAZY MURDER ATTEMPT.

THE WOMAN FINDS HER SON DYING AND STARTS RUNNING AROUND THE TOWN SCREAMING, SO ISIS COMES TO THE RESCUE AND MAGICS THE BOY BACK TO LIFE.

SHE DOESN'T PUNISH THE SCORPIONS AT ALL THOUGH. ISIS REALLY DOESN'T GIVE A SHIT ABOUT ANYTHING, SHE JUST COULDN'T SLEEP BECAUSE OF THE SCREAMING.

SPHINX SURPRISE

THUTMOSE, THE PRINCE OF EGYPT, HAS FUCKED UP BIG-TIME. HE DID SOMETHING FUCKING STUPID (NOBODY HAS A FUCKING CLUE WHAT), AND NOW EVERYBODY HATES HIM AND THINKS HE'LL NEVER BE PHARAOH. HIS LIFE IS PRETTY FUCKING SHIT, AND HE'S FUCKING MISERABLE.

THUTMOSE GOES FOR A WALK, BECAUSE EVERYTHING IS SHIT AND HE WANTS TO GO AND CRY IN THE DESERT. HE WALKS FOR ABOUT THREE DAYS, AND THEN HE JUST SITS ON THE FLOOR AND CRIES. SUDDENLY, THERE'S A MOTHERFUCKING EARTHQUAKE. THUTMOSE FALLS OVER AND SHITS HIMSELF IN TERROR AS A FUCKING MASSIVE STONE SPHINX BURSTS OUT OF THE GROUND IN FRONT OF HIM.

THE STONE SPHINX STARES AT HIM AND SHOUTS "SURPRISE, BITCH! I'M YOUR DAD!"

THUTMOSE TELLS THE SPHINX TO FUCK OFF, BECAUSE LAST TIME HE CHECKED HIS DAD DIDN'T SPEND HIS SPARE TIME BURIED IN THE DESERT. OH, AND HE WASN'T TEN FUCKING FEET TALL AND MADE OF STONE. ALSO HE HAD PEOPLE LEGS NOT FUCKING LION LEGS.

THE SPHINX LOOKS A BIT AWKWARD AND ADMITS THAT IT MEANT THAT IN A COMPLICATED AS FUCK METAPHORICAL SENSE, BUT THAT DOESN'T MATTER. THEN IT EXPLAINS TO THUTMOSE THAT HE SHOULD STOP BEING SUCH A WHINY LITTLE BITCH BECAUSE HE'S GOING TO BE THE FUCKING PHARAOH SOON ENOUGH.

THUTMOSE ACCEPTS THIS BLINDLY AND STOPS CRYING, BECAUSE ALL THE REASSURANCE HE NEEDS IS SOME ADVICE FROM A GIANT STATUE PRETENDING TO BE HIS DAD. THUTMOSE IS A GULLIBLE LITTLE SHIT, BUT HE DOES EVENTUALLY BECOME PHARAOH.

MAYBE YOU SHOULD PAY ATTENTION TO SURPRISING SPHINXES THAT LIE ABOUT BEING FAMILY MEMBERS. WHO FUCKING KNOWS.

DON'T STEAL FROM THE GODS

THOTH, THE GOD OF WISDOM, HAS A BOOK OF FUCKING MAGIC SPELLS. HE KEEPS IT IN A BOX WRAPPED IN AN IMMORTAL SNAKE, BURIED IN A HOLE IN THE DESERT FUCKING MILES AWAY FROM CIVILISATION.

PRINCE NEFREKEPTAH DECIDES HE WANTS TO BE A MOTHERFUCKING WIZARD, SO HE SETS OFF INTO THE DESERT TO FIND THE MAGIC BOOK AND STEAL THE SHIT OUT OF IT.

EVENTUALLY HE FINDS WHERE THE MAGIC BOOK IS BURIED. UNFORTUNATELY, IT'S SURROUNDED BY FUCKLOADS OF SNAKES AND MOTHERFUCKING SCORPIONS. THE SNAKES AND SCORPIONS ARE REALLY SHIT AT THEIR JOB, THOUGH, AND THEY DON'T GIVE A FUCK ABOUT NEFREKEPTAH. HE WALKS RIGHT THROUGH THEM AND POKES THE IMMORTAL SERPENT GUARDING THE BOX IN THE FACE.

THE SNAKE IS PRETTY FUCKING FURIOUS, AND IT DIVES AT NEFREKEPTAH, WHO JUST FUCKING BEHEADS IT. BEING AN IMMORTAL SNAKE, THOUGH, IT DOESN'T FUCKING DIE. THE HEAD FLIES BACK ONTO THE BODY AND THE SNAKE TRIES AGAIN. ONCE AGAIN, NEFREKEPTAH BEATS THE SHIT OUT OF THE SNAKE, BUT THIS TIME HE THROWS THE HEAD IN THE RIVER. THAT DOESN'T STOP IT FROM REATTACHING, THOUGH, AND HE HAS TO DO IT ALL OVER AGAIN. NEXT TIME, HE POURS A BUCKET OF SAND OVER THE STUMP, AND THE HEAD JUST BOUNCES OFF. HE LEAVES THE SNAKE WRIGGLING AROUND ON THE FLOOR WITH ITS HEAD BOUNCING EVERYWHERE, OPENS THE BOX, GRABS THE MAGIC BOOK, AND FUCKS OFF.

UNFORTUNATELY FOR NEFREKEPTAH, THOTH REALISES THE BOOK'S BEEN STOLEN AND MURDERS HIM, HIS WIFE AND ALL HIS CHILDREN. YOU REALLY SHOULDN'T PISS OFF THE GODS. THEY CAN GET STABBY AS FUCK.

NORSE MYTHOLOGY

BEGINNINGS: NORSE STYLE

IN THE BEGINNING THERE IS ONLY ICE AND FIRE AND FUCKING NOTHINGNESS. THEN THE ICE STARTS MELTING AND THE GIANT YMIR FUCKING PLOPS OUT OF IT. HE THEN SWEATS OUT MORE FUCKING GIANTS FROM HIS SWEATY PORES - THIS SHIT IS NASTY OK?

HE'S BEST BUDDIES WITH A FUCKING COW, AND THEY HAVE A FUCKING HAPPY LITTLE LIFE TOGETHER LIKE SOME SORT OF BULLSHIT CARTOON UNTIL THE COW LICKS AWAY AT THE ICE AND A GOD FALLS OUT OF IT. OOPS. COWS ARE ALL STUPID BASTARDS.

BURI IS THE FIRST OF THE AESIR, THE MAIN GOD FAMILY WITH ALL THE FAMOUS FUCKERS IN IT. BURI GETS BUSY AND SOON HE HAS CHILDREN AND THEN GRANDKIDS; ODIN AND HIS TWO BROTHERS (VILI AND VE) WHO HE KIND OF FUCKING OVER-SHADOWS.

THEN, FOR COMPLETELY NO REASON, ODIN AND HIS BROS FUCKING MURDER YMIR. ASSHOLES. THIS ASSHOLERY ALLOWED THEM TO CUT HIS FUCKING BODY UP AND MAKE THE WORLD WITH IT (THE SKY IS MADE FROM YMIR'S SKULL, DIDN'T YOU FUCKERS KNOW?).

MORAL OF THE STORY: SENSELESS MURDER IS O-FUCKING-KAY AS LONG AS IT'S CONSTRUCTIVE SHIT.

LOKI IS A SHIT STYLIST

ONE DAY LOKI IS BEING A GINORMOUS SHITWEASEL AND DECIDES TO CUT OFF ALL OF SIF'S FUCKING HAIR. WHAT A DICK. SIF'S HUSBAND THOR IS PRETTY PISSED OFF BY THIS, SO THREATENS TO BEAT THE CRAP OUT OF LOKI UNLESS HE FIXES HIS FUCK-UP.

SO LOKI GOES TO GET SOME NEW HAIR FOR SIF...FROM THE DWARVES, NORSE MYTHOLOGY'S GREATEST FUCKING HAIR STYLISTS. THE DWARVES MAKE SOME NEW HAIR FROM GOLD, AND ALSO A HANDY FOLDING BOAT AND A BADASS SPEAR. FUCKING SERVICE RIGHT THERE.

BEING THE COMPLETE FUCKING ASSHOLE HE IS, LOKI JUST STAYS WITH THE DWARVES AND DICKS AROUND WITH THEM FOR A BIT, AND TRICKS THEM INTO MAKING MORE NICE THINGS (LIKE THOR'S FUCKING HAMMER, MJOLNIR. ALSO A GOLD PIG, BUT THAT'S NOT QUITE AS USEFUL).

LOKI RETURNS HOME AND GIVES OUT THESE GIFTS TO THE OTHER GODS, AND EVERYONE IS FUCKING HAPPY. EXCEPT THE DWARVES WHOM LOKI HAD FUCKED OVER. SO THEY SEW THE LITTLE SHIT'S MOUTH SHUT. ASSHOLES. HE DESERVES IT, BUT THEY'RE STILL A BUNCH OF FUCKING DICKBAGS.

THOR LOOKS FUCKING MAGNIFICENT IN A DRESS

ONE DAY, THOR REALISES HIS FUCKING HAMMER, MJOLNIR, HAS GONE. HE'S NATURALLY PRETTY FUCKING PISSED OFF ABOUT THIS (AS HE ALWAYS IS). THE FUCKING GIANTS HAVE STOLEN IT, THE LITTLE SHITS. EXCEPT THEY'RE GIANTS SO THEY'RE PRETTY FUCKING MASSIVE SHITS. THE GODS SEND LOKI OVER TO JOTUNHEIM (THE GIANTS' HANG-OUT) TO FIND OUT WHICH ASSHOLE IN PARTICULAR HAS THE FUCKING MAGICAL DIY TOOL.

OF COURSE IT'S THE CHIEF GIANT (THRYM) WHO'S DONE THE THIEVERY, AND OF FUCKING COURSE HE'S BURIED IT EIGHT FUCKING MILES UNDERGROUND. AND HE'S SO FOREVER-ALONE THAT HE SAYS HE'LL ONLY GIVE IT BACK IF HE GETS TO MARRY FREYA (SUPER SEXY LOVE GODDESS). FREYA IS NOT FUCKING HAPPY WITH THIS. WHO WANTS TO MARRY A FUCKING UGLY GIANT ANYWAY?

THEN ONE OF THE GODS SUGGESTS THE CUNNING PLAN OF DRESSING THOR UP AS FREYA AND SENDING HIM OVER AS A FAKE HOSTAGE. FUCK YES, THOR IN A DRESS. THE GODS MAKE HIM LOOK AS PRETTY AS POSSIBLE, WITH MAKE UP AND FLOWERS AND SPARKLES AND BULLSHIT LIKE THAT. FOR A FUCKING MASSIVE DUDE WITH A BEARD HE DOESN'T LOOK FUCKING BAD AT ALL. THEN LOKI SAYS HE WANTS IN ON THE PLOT (SHENANIGANS LIKE THIS ARE HIS FAVOURITE FUCKING THING) AND COMES ALONG AS THOR'S MAID (THOUGH PROBABLY JUST TO FUCKING LAUGH AT HIM LIKE THE ASSHOLE HE IS).

THE GIANTS TOTALLY ACCEPT THOR'S SEXY DRESS, AND EVERYTHING IS GOING JUST FUCKING FINE. UNTIL, AT THE WELCOMING FEAST, THOR JUST EATS FUCKING EVERYTHING, IN A VERY UNLADYLIKE MANNER. BUT GIANTS ARE GENERALLY FUCKING STUPID SO LOKI MANAGES TO LIE THEIR WAY OUT OF THIS BY MAKING UP SOME STUPID BULLSHIT.

FINALLY, AFTER THRYM HAS BROUGHT MJOLLNIR UP (TO FUCKING SHOW OFF, NO DOUBT), HE PUTS THOR IN HIS LAP AND STARTS GETTING TOUCHY FEELY. THOR IS COMPLETELY NOT DOWN FOR THIS, AND JUST GRABS HIS HAMMER AND SLAUGHTERS FUCKING EVERYONE.

HE THEN PRESUMABLY TAKES HIS SLINKY DRESS OFF, BUT WE LIKE TO THINK HE KEEPS IT AROUND FOR SPECIAL FUCKING OCCASIONS.

LOKI IS A FUCKING SEXY HORSE

THERE'S A FUCKING MASSIVE BATTLE, AND ALL THE WALLS AROUND ASGARD GET KNOCKED DOWN. THAT LEAVES THE GODS PRETTY FUCKING VULNERABLE TO ATTACK FROM THE GIANTS, WHO ARE REALLY SHITTY GUYS.

CONVENIENTLY, A STONEMASON CALLED BLAST (WHICH IS A FUCKING STUPID NAME) SHOWS UP AND SAYS HE'LL FIX THE WALLS BUT HE WANTS PAYING IN WOMEN. SPECIFICALLY, HE WANTS TO MARRY FREYA. HE'S A DICK. FORTUNATELY, LOKI HAS A CUNNING PLAN. HE HAGGLES THE FUCKING MASON DOWN TO AN AGREEMENT THAT HE CAN HAVE FREYA IF HE FINISHES THE JOB WITHIN SIX MONTHS WITH NOTHING BUT A MOTHERFUCKING HORSE TO HELP HIM.

IT GETS TO THE LAST DAY, AND IT LOOKS LIKE THE STONEMASON MIGHT FINISH THE FUCKING JOB AFTER ALL. THE AESIR ARE PRETTY FUCKING FURIOUS AT LOKI, BUT HE DOESN'T GIVE A SHIT. HE HAS A PLAN. LOKI ALWAYS HAS A PLAN.

LOKI TURNS INTO A HORSE. A SEXY HORSE. THAT'S RIGHT, HE TURNS INTO A FUCKING HORSE. THEN HE SEDUCES BLAST'S HORSE. THEY HAVE HORSEY SEX ALL NIGHT AND THAT KEEPS THE HORSE SO DISTRACTED THAT THE JOB ISN'T FINISHED IN TIME AND THE POOR STONEMASON GOES WITHOUT PAY. ALL THE AESIR ARE DICKS.

NINE MONTHS LATER, LOKI VANISHES INTO THE WOODS AND COMES BACK WITH A BABY HORSE. IT'S GOT EIGHT LEGS. IT'S A MOTHERFUCKING SPIDER HORSE. ALSO IT CAN FLY.

YES, THAT'S RIGHT. LOKI SLEEPS WITH A HORSE AND THEN GIVES BIRTH TO A MAGIC FLYING HORSE BABY. NORSE MYTHOLOGY IS FUCKING WEIRD.

THOR AND LOKI GO ON A GIANT ADVENTURE

ONE DAY, THOR GETS REALLY FUCKING BORED. WHEN THOR GETS BORED, HE WANTS TO BEAT PEOPLE AT STUPID BULLSHIT, BECAUSE THOR'S A DICK.

THOR AND LOKI GET ON THEIR HORSES AND SET OFF TO UTGARD, WHERE THE MOTHERFUCKING GIANTS LIVE, BECAUSE THOR THINKS THEY MIGHT BE A BIT OF A CHALLENGE, AND ALSO BECAUSE THOR LIKES BEATING UP GIANTS.

THEY GET TO UTGARD, AND THE GIANTS LET THEM IN. THOR DECLARES THAT HE WANTS TO BEAT THEM ALL AT STUPID BULLSHIT, AND THEY AGREE.

THE GIANTS SET THOR SOME NICE EASY CHALLENGES. FIRST UP, HE HAS TO DOWN A HORN FULL OF MEAD IN ONE.

HE CAN'T DO IT.

SECOND, HE HAS TO PICK UP A CAT.

HE CAN'T DO IT. THOR CAN'T PICK UP A FUCKING CAT.

THIRD, HE HAS TO WRESTLE SOMEONE'S GRANDMA.

GUESS WHAT, MOTHERFUCKERS? HE CAN'T DO IT. THOR GETS BEATEN IN A WRESTLING MATCH BY A LITTLE OLD GRANDMA. THOR IS REALLY SHIT.

THOR LEAVES IN A MASSIVE SULK BECAUSE HE CAN'T STAND LOSING, BUT THEN THE KING OF THE GIANTS COMES OUT AND LAUGHS AT HIM. THE GIANTS FUCKING CHEATED. THE HORN WASN'T FULL OF MEAD, IT WAS JUST CONNECTED TO THE SEA. THOR CAN'T TELL THE DIFFERENCE BETWEEN SEAWATER AND MEAD. WHAT A FUCKING IDIOT.

THE CAT WASN'T ACTUALLY A CAT, IT WAS ACTUALLY JORMUNGAND, THE GIANT SNAKE THAT GOES ALL AROUND THE WORLD.

THE GRANDMA WAS ACTUALLY OLD AGE ITSELF.

IT'S ALL FUCKING BULLSHIT AND THOR GRABS HIS HAMMER TO KILL THE GIANTS, BUT WHEN HE TURNS ROUND THEY'VE ALL MAGICALLY VANISHED. NEEDLESS TO SAY, THOR IS FUCKING FURIOUS. HE PROBABLY TAKES IT ALL OUT ON LOKI LATER, BECAUSE LOKI'S JUST BEEN WATCHING AND LAUGHING ALL THE WAY THROUGH. LOKI'S A DICK TOO.

DON'T FUCK AROUND WITH MISTLETOE

BALDUR IS ONE OF THE FEW NICE GUYS OF NORSE MYTHOLOGY, SO WHEN THIS CUTIE STARTS GETTING BAD DREAMS ABOUT HIS DEATH, HIS DADDY ODIN GOES TO FIND OUT WHAT THE FUCK IS GOING ON.

SOME TRIPPY-ASS PROPHET (NOT A TRIPPY ASS-PROPHET. THAT'S A COMPLETELY FUCKING DIFFERENT SORT OF THING) TELLS HIM THAT BALDUR WILL BE KILLED BY HIS BROTHER HODR WITH SOME FUCKING TWIG. BALDUR'S MUMMY FRIGGA IS FUCKING ANGRY ABOUT THIS SHIT SO SHE MAKES EVERY SINGLE THING IN THE ENTIRE FUCKING NINE WORLDS PROMISE NOT TO HURT CUTE LIL BALDUR.

THE GODS THEN FUCKING THROW STONES AND SHIT AT BALDUR TO TEST WHETHER HE'LL BE SAFE. HE'S FUCKING FINE, STONES KEEP THEIR PROMISES. THIS PISSES OFF LOKI BECAUSE HE WANTS MORE SHIT TO BE HITTING THE FAN. SO HE GETS FRIGGA TO ADMIT THAT SHE FORGOT TO MAKE ONE LITTLE PIECE OF SHIT PROMISE TO NOT HURT BALDUR; MOTHERFUCKING MISTLETOE.

NATURALLY LOKI FUCKS OFF AND BUYS A SHIT TONNE OF MISTLETOE, AND GOES BACK TO WHERE ALL THE GODS ARE RANDOMLY CHUCKING THINGS AT BALDUR. PRETENDING TO BE A FUCKING REASONABLE GUY AND HELPING A BLIND DUDE ENJOY THE HEALTHY VIOLENT FUN, LOKI HANDS SOME MISTLETOE TO THE BLIND GOD HODR, AND HELPS HIM AIM.

HODR THROWS THE MISTLETOE RIGHT AT BALDUR. IT GOES STRAIGHT FUCKING THROUGH HIM AND HE DIES. IT'S SUPER FUCKING AWKWARD. DON'T WORRY THOUGH, BALDUR IS SUPPOSED TO RETURN SOMEDAY BEFORE THE END OF THE WORLD, BUT IN THE MEAN TIME, DON'T FUCK AROUND WITH MISTLETOE THIS HOLIDAY SEASON: THAT SHIT IS DANGEROUS.

THE VOLSUNGSAGA

THE VOLSUNGSAGA IS PRETTY FUCKING GREAT. IT'S GOT DRAGONS AND MURDER AND SHIT LIKE THAT. IT'S ALSO WHAT THE LORD OF THE RINGS WAS INSPIRED BY.

SO ONE DAY ODIN HEARS A PROPHECY THAT IF A HUMAN DRAGONSLAYER WHO IS ALSO HIS SON JOINS HIM IN VALHALLA THEN THE WORLD WON'T END. WHAT DOES ODIN DO?

THAT'S RIGHT, HE HAS A WANK AND MAGICALLY IMPREGNATES ABOUT A MILLION PEOPLE ALL OVER THE WORLD. LOTS OF HEROES DIE AND GO TO VALHALLA, BUT THEY'RE ALL SHIT AND NONE OF THEM HAVE KILLED DRAGONS. ODIN'S GETTING PRETTY FUCKING WORRIED.

MEANWHILE, A CRAZY DWARF CALLED ANDVARI MAKES A HUGE PILE OF TREASURE, INCLUDING A RING. NO, IT DOESN'T TURN PEOPLE INVISIBLE, IT'S JUST A FUCKING RING. LOKI, NEEDING FUCKLOADS OF GOLD TO PAY OFF A RANSOM FOR A STUNT THAT WENT WRONG, BLACKMAILS ANDVARI INTO GIVING HIM ALL THE TREASURE EXCEPT THE RING. HE JUST STEALS THE RING. ANDVARI IS PRETTY FUCKING PISSED OFF, AND CURSES THE RING SO ANYONE THAT OWNS IT WILL DIE.

ALSO, SOME CRAZY MAGIC VIKINGS HAVE MADE A MAGIC SWORD THAT HAS TO BE PULLED OUT OF A TREE AND NOBODY EXCEPT A GREAT HERO CAN DO IT. IT'S A SHITTY SWORD THOUGH, AND ENDS UP GETTING BROKEN.

ALL THESE PLOT THREADS WILL PAY OFF LATER, DON'T FUCKING WORRY.

ONE DAY, A GUY CALLED SIGURD DECIDES HE'S GOING TO GO AND KILL A DRAGON. ONE PROBLEM: HIS FATHER'S MAGIC SWORD IS BROKEN (SOUND FAMILIAR?). HE GETS IT REFORGED THOUGH, AND NOW HE'S ALL SET TO GO DRAGON-MURDERING.

HE WAITS FOR FAFNIR THE DRAGON (WHO'S ACTUALLY HIS MAGIC STEP-UNCLE OR SOME CRAZY SHIT LIKE THAT) TO GO FOR A DRINK, THEN HIDES IN A HOLE IN THE GROUND AND WAITS FOR HIM TO COME HOME FROM THE DRAGON PUB. WHEN FAFNIR (WHO'S EXACTLY LIKE SMAUG FROM THE HOBBIT JUST BIGGER AND ANGRIER) COMES HOME, SIGURD STABS HIM FROM UNDERNEATH AND HE DIES. IT'S KIND OF PATHETIC. ALL THE BLOOD GOES ALL OVER SIGURD, WHO IS NOW MAGICALLY STAB-PROOF. THEN HE JUMPS OUT IN FRONT OF THE DYING DRAGON AND THEY HAVE AN ARGUMENT. IT'S PRETTY SHITTY, FAFNIR JUST TRIES TO WARN SIGURD ABOUT MAGIC BULLSHIT AND SIGURD TELLS HIM TO FUCK OFF. LATER SIGURD EATS FAFNIR'S HEART, WHICH LETS HIM TALK TO BIRDS. BASICALLY THE SHITTIEST SUPERPOWER EVER.

THEN SIGURD STEALS ALL THE FUCKING TREASURE. INCLUDING A CERTAIN CURSED RING, WHICH HE NATURALLY DECIDES IS GREAT AND PUTS ON, COMPLETELY IGNORING ALL OF FAFNIR'S WARNINGS. LIFE TIP: PAY ATTENTION TO ADVICE FROM DRAGONS.

SIGURD IS NOW THE PROPHECIED DRAGON SLAYER, AND ALSO MAGICALLY INDESTRUCTIBLE. AND ALSO A DICK, BUT THAT'S JUST WHAT HAPPENS WHEN YOU'RE A HERO. ALL HE'S MISSING IS A WOMAN, SO HE SETS OFF ON HIS MAGIC HORSE TO GO AND STEAL A PRINCESS.

SIGURD, THE MAGIC STAB PROOF DRAGON SLAYING HALF GOD WITH A MAGIC SWORD, A MAGIC HORSE, A CURSED RING, AND NO MORALS AT ALL, IS LOOKING FOR A PRINCESS TO RUN OFF WITH. FORTUNATELY, THE BIRDS TELL HIM ABOUT A CONVENIENT ONE. CONVENIENT, IN THIS CASE, MEANS "TRAPPED BEHIND A RING OF FIRE AND LIGHTNING, CHAINED TO THE TOP OF A MOUNTAIN". OH YES, AND SHE'S ALSO A VALKYRIE.

SIGURD'S MAGIC HORSE JUMPS OVER THE FIRE AND LIGHTNING, HE CUTS THE CHAINS, AND THEN THE VALKYRIE (BRUNHILDE)

PROMISES TO MARRY HIM. ON CONDITION THAT HE CAN GET HIMSELF A FUCKING KINGDOM OF HIS VERY OWN.

WHAT DOES SIGURD DO? HE PROMISES TO COME BACK SOON AND FUCKS OFF TO FIND A KINGDOM, LEAVING HER TO HER OWN DEVICES FOR AS LONG AS IT TAKES. WHAT A DICK.

HE GOES TO THE KINGDOM OF WORMS (YES, THAT REALLY IS ITS NAME. SHUT THE FUCK UP), AND IS IMMEDIATELY FED A LOVE POTION BY THE EVIL WITCH QUEEN AND MARRIES THE PRINCESS, FORGETTING ALL ABOUT BRUNHILDE. IT'S ALL LOOKING PRETTY SHITTY.

SIGURD'S BEEN TRICKED INTO MARRYING PRINCESS GUDRUN, SO BRUNHILDE THE VALKYRIE IS STUCK ON TOP OF A MOUNTAIN ON HER OWN. NATURALLY, A FUCKING MASSIVE CIRCLE OF FIRE SURROUNDS HER, SO SHE'S LITERALLY STUCK THERE UNTIL HER MAGIC FIREPROOF FIANCE COMES HOME. THE PROBLEM IS, HE'S MARRIED TO SOMEONE ELSE AND HAS FORGOTTEN ALL ABOUT BRUNHILDE. SIGURD IS A BIT OF A DICK AND ALSO A COMPLETE IDIOT.

THE EVIL QUEEN WHO MADE SIGURD MARRY GUDRUN THEN DECIDES HER BROTHER GUNNAR SHOULD MARRY BRUNHILDE. ONE PROBLEM: GUNNAR ISN'T MAGIC AND FIREPROOF. SHE MAGICS SIGURD TO LOOK LIKE GUNNAR AND MAKES HIM MARRY BRUNHILDE, THEN THEY SWITCH HIM FOR THE REAL GUNNAR. IT'S PRETTY FUCKING CONFUSING.

THE NEXT MORNING, BRUNHILDE WAKES UP AND SEES SIGURD SITTING NEXT TO GUDRUN. UNDERSTANDABLY, SHE'S FUCKING FURIOUS. THEN THE SPELL WEARS OFF AND SIGURD REALISES WHAT HE'S DONE.

WHOOPS.

BRUNHILDE GOES CRAZY AND STABS SIGURD. HE'S STAB PROOF BECAUSE HE HAD A SHOWER IN DRAGON'S BLOOD, BUT UNFORTUNATELY THERE WAS A LEAF ON HIS BACK SO HE HAS

A PATCH WHERE HE'S ALL SQUISHY. BRUNHILDE GETS REALLY FUCKING LUCKY AND STABS HIM IN THE SQUISHY BIT, AND HE DIES.

THEN SHE REALISES WHAT SHE'S DONE, STABS HERSELF, AND JUMPS ON HIS FUNERAL PYRE. IT'S VERY AENEID IV, BUT WITH MORE BETRAYAL AND TWICE AS MANY CORPSES.

GUDRUN THEN WANDERS ROUND AND ROUND IN CIRCLES BEING SAD FOR YEARS, BEFORE THROWING HERSELF OFF A CLIFF. NOW EVERYONE'S DEAD, WHICH IS THE TRADITIONAL ENDING TO MOST NORSE MYTHS.

SEALS ARE SLIPPERY LITTLE SHITS

FREYA HAS A MAGIC NECKLACE. IT'S CALLED BRISINGAMEN AND IT'S FUCKING USELESS. ONE DAY, SHE GOES TO SLEEP, AND WHEN SHE WAKES UP IT'S GONE. WHO COULD POSSIBLY HAVE TAKEN IT? COULD IT POSSIBLY HAVE BEEN LOKI?

NO. IT WAS A MOTHERFUCKING SEAL.

ACTUALLY IT WAS LOKI IN THE FORM OF A SEAL, BUT STILL. FREYA'S NECKLACE GOT STOLEN BY A SEAL AND SHE DIDN'T FUCKING NOTICE. HOW STUPID CAN YOU GET?

FREYA GOES TO ASK HEIMDALL FOR HELP, BECAUSE HEIMDALL IS THE CLOSEST THING TO A POLICEMAN THAT THE AESIR HAVE. HEIMDALL IS REALLY CLOSER TO SOME SORT OF FUCKED UP BOND VILLAIN THOUGH; HE CAN HEAR THE GRASS GROW, HE HAS NINE MOTHERS, GOLDEN TEETH, AND A FUCKING MASSIVE TRUMPET. HEIMDALL AND FREYA GO ON AN ADVENTURE TO FIND LOKI THE SEAL AND BEAT THE SHIT OUT OF HIM.

WHEN THEY EVENTUALLY FIND THE THIEF, HEIMDALL GETS READY TO BEAT THE SHIT OUT OF HIM. HE COULD JUST STAB HIM; SEALS AREN'T KNOWN FOR THEIR MARTIAL PROWESS. THAT WOULD BE TOO EASY THOUGH, AND HEIMDALL IS FUCKING INSANE. INSTEAD, HE TURNS INTO A SEAL TOO AND THEY HAVE A FIGHT. A FUCKING SEAL FIGHT. THEY JUST SIT THERE IN THE WATER SLAPPING EACH OTHER AND GOING "ARF ARF" ANGRILY. FREYA BEGINS TO WONDER WHAT THE FUCK SHE THOUGHT SHE WAS DOING BRINGING A CRAZY BASTARD LIKE HEIMDALL ALONG, BUT IN THE END HE WINS BY SEAL-SLAPPING LOKI INTO UNCONSCIOUSNESS AND GETS FREYA BACK HER NECKLACE.

NEVER TRUST A SEAL.

ODIN IS SHIT WITH BABIES

IN ANOTHER FIT OF REBELLION, LOKI GETS ANGRBODA, A GIANTESS, PREGNANT. BECAUSE HE'S MOTHERFUCKING LOKI, HOWEVER, SHE DOESN'T JUST HAVE NORMAL BABIES. INSTEAD, SHE GIVES BIRTH TO MONSTERS.

THERE'S FENRIR, WHO'S A FUCKING MASSIVE WOLF MONSTER, JORMUNGAND, WHO'S A FUCKING MASSIVE SNAKE MONSTER, AND HEL. HEL'S NOT A FUCKING MASSIVE MONSTER, SHE'S JUST KIND OF BLACK AND MELTY DOWN ONE SIDE.

EVENTUALLY, ODIN FINDS OUT THAT LOKI'S GOT BABIES BEING BROUGHT UP SOMEWHERE IN JOTUNHEIM, AND DEMANDS THAT HE BRINGS THEM TO ASGARD FOR BABY INSPECTION.

LOKI RELUCTANTLY BRINGS THE BABIES TO ASGARD FOR ODIN TO INSPECT, AND ODIN ISN'T VERY IMPRESSED. HIS REACTION IS ALONG THE LINES OF "WHAT THE FUCK LOKI. THOSE AREN'T NORMAL BABIES. THAT'S A PUPPY AND A SNAKE AND A REALLY FUCKING UGLY MELTY BABY." THEN HE THROWS JORMUNGAND OUT OF THE WINDOW INTO THE SEA, THROWS HEL TO NIFLHEIM (THE NORSE UNDERWORLD), AND STICKS FENRIR IN A MAGIC KENNEL.

ODIN IS, AS ALWAYS, A DICK, AND HE HAS NO IDEA HOW TO DEAL WITH BABIES. LOKI'S A SHIT DAD, BUT ODIN'S WORSE.

DON'T FEED THE GIANT DEMON WOLF MONSTER

AFTER ODIN'S KIDNAPPED LOKI'S DEMON WOLF SON FENRIR AND STUCK HIM IN A KENNEL, THINGS ARE A BIT COMPLICATED IN ASGARD. FENRIR'S NOT A VERY WELL BEHAVED ANGRY DEMON WOLF MONSTER. ACTUALLY, HE'S A VICIOUS LITTLE SHIT. IN ORDER TO DEAL WITH HIM PROPERLY, THE AESIR DECIDE TO PUT A MAGIC COLLAR ON HIM. SORT OF LIKE A CONE OF SHAME, BUT MADE OF METAL AND MAGIC. THE AESIR ARE ALL DICKS.

FENRIR DOESN'T TRUST THEM, FOR GOOD REASON, SO HE REFUSES TO HAVE THE COLLAR PUT ON HIM WITHOUT SOME SORT OF INSURANCE. PROMISING THAT THEY JUST NEED TO DO A TEST FIT AND THEY'LL LET FENRIR GO AFTERWARDS (FUCKING LIARS), THE AESIR MANAGE TO PERSUADE TYR TO STICK HIS HAND IN FENRIR'S MOUTH AS "INSURANCE".

TYR SHOVES HIS HAND IN FENRIR'S MOUTH, AND THEN THE AESIR STICK THE COLLAR ON FENRIR AND ALL FUCK OFF. FENRIR AND TYR ARE BOTH PRETTY FUCKING FURIOUS, AS THEY'VE BEEN TRICKED, BUT FENRIR'S THE ONE WITH FUCKING MASSIVE POINTY TEETH. TYR GETS HIS HAND BITTEN OFF, AND THEN NOBODY'S HAPPY. IT'S ALL KIND OF SHIT REALLY.

BALDUR'S FUCKED UP FUNERAL

AFTER BALDUR HAS HIS LITTLE "ACCIDENT" WITH THE MISTLETOE, EVERYONE IS COMPLETELY FUCKING MISERABLE. TO START WITH, ODIN HAS A REVENGE BABY WITH A GIANTESS. THE BABY GROWS TO ADULTHOOD WITHIN A DAY, MURDERS HODR (BALDUR'S KILLER), AND THEN GETS ABANDONED ONTO THE STREETS. ODIN'S A DICK.

THEN, THE AESIR PUT BALDUR'S BODY ON HIS BOAT, WHICH IS THE BIGGEST BOAT IN THE WORLD, AND SET FIRE TO IT. THEN THEY TRY TO PUSH IT OUT TO SEA, BUT IT'S TOO FUCKING BIG AND HEAVY AND THEY CAN'T DO IT. SHIT.

WHILE THEY'RE TRYING TO FIND SOMEONE STRONG ENOUGH TO PUSH THE BURNING BOAT OUT TO SEA, EVERYONE USES IT AS A STANDERD MYTHOLOGICAL FUNERAL PYRE. BALDUR'S WIFE NANNA DIES OF GRIEF THEN THROWS HERSELF ONTO THE PYRE. OR THROWS HERSELF ONTO THE PYRE THEN DIES OF GRIEF. OR JUST DIES OF BEING ON FUCKING FIRE. IT DEPENDS WHICH SOURCE YOU LOOK AT.

THEN SOMEONE THROWS BALDUR'S FUCKING HORSE ONTO THE PYRE AND IT BURNS TO DEATH. NOT TO BE OUTDONE, THOR KICKS A DWARF CALLED LITT ONTO THE PYRE AND HE BURNS TO DEATH TOO. THOR'S A DICK. THIS IS AN ACHILLES-LEVEL DISPLAY OF BEING A DICK WITH A FUNERAL PYRE.

FORTUNATELY, BEFORE ANYONE ELSE CAN BURN TO DEATH, A GIANTESS CALLED HYRROKIN SHOWS UP RIDING A MOTHERFUCKING WOLF AND PUSHES THE BOAT OUT TO SEA.

124

LOKI IS A FUCKING AWFUL DRUNK

THE SEA (AND BEER) GOD AEGIR DECIDES TO HAVE A FUCKING MASSIVE PARTY, AND INVITES ALL THE OTHER GODS. HIS SERVANTS, ELDIR AND FIMAFENG, OPEN THE DOORS FOR EVERYONE. UNFORTUNATELY FOR THEM, LOKI HAS BEEN PRE-DRINKING. WHAT A FUCKING DICK. HE SHOWS UP DRUNK AND STABS FIMAFENG AS SOON AS HE OPENS THE DOOR, WHICH IS A DICK MOVE HOWEVER YOU LOOK AT IT. ALL THE OTHER GODS ARE PRETTY FUCKING ANGRY, WHICH IS PERFECTLY REASONABLE GIVEN THE SHIT LOKI'S JUST DONE, AND THROW HIM OUT OF THE PARTY.

LOKI SNEAKS UP TO THE BACK DOOR, WHERE ELDIR TELLS HIM THAT ALL THE OTHER GODS ARE GETTING WASTED WITHOUT HIM AND HE SHOULD PROBABLY FUCK OFF NOW. LOKI TELLS ELDIR TO FUCK OFF AND THEN RUNS PAST HIM INTO THE HALL.

BY THIS STAGE, EVERYONE IS DRUNK, SO THEY DON'T NOTICE LOKI RUN IN AND SIT DOWN, AND BY THE TIME THEY SPOT HIM IT'S TOO LATE. LOKI STANDS UP AND MAKES A TOAST TO EVERYONE EXCEPT BRAGI, WHO GETS REALLY FUCKING UPSET. HE THINKS HE'S OFFENDED LOKI, SO HE OFFERS HIM A HORSE AND A BUCKET OF GOLD. LOKI TELLS BRAGI TO FUCK OFF UNLESS HE'LL OFFER HIM HIS WIFE, AND BRAGI THREATENS TO HIT HIM. THEN LOKI INSULTS EVERYONE ELSE, BUT HE DOESN'T GIVE A FUCK ABOUT THEIR THREATS OF VIOLENCE.

SOME TIME LATER, THOR SHOWS UP TO FIND LOKI BEING RUDE ABOUT EVERYONE'S MOTHERS AND EVERYONE ELSE CRYING ON THE FLOOR BECAUSE THEY CAN'T DO ANYTHING. THOR, BEING A PRETTY SENSIBLE MOTHERFUCKER, TELLS LOKI HE'LL SMACK HIM IN THE FACE WITH A HAMMER SO HARD HIS HEAD'LL FALL OFF.

LOKI QUITE LIKES HIS HEAD, SO HE FUCKS OFF, HAVING FUCKED UP THE PARTY COMPLETELY FOR EVERYONE ELSE.

ODIN IS SHIT AT DATING

ODIN FALLS IN LOVE WITH A DWARF LADY. SHE HAS A LUXURIANT AND FLUFFY BEARD, AND HE THINKS THAT'S FUCKING HOT.

UNFORTUNATELY FOR ODIN, THE SEXY DWARF LADY DOESN'T LIKE HIM BACK, AND REJECTS HIM. ODIN DOESN'T TAKE NO FOR A FUCKING ANSWER, THOUGH, BECAUSE HE'S A FUCKING DICK, AND KEEPS HITTING ON HER.

IN THE END, SHE GIVES IN AND TELLS HIM TO COME TO HER HOUSE IN THE MIDDLE OF THE NIGHT FOR STEAMY BEARD SEX. ODIN SHOWS UP TO FIND THE HOUSE SURROUNDED BY ANGRY MEN WITH SWORDS AND BURNING TORCHES, ALL READY TO FUCK HIM UP. ODIN FUCKS OFF, BECAUSE HE REALLY DOESN'T WANT TO BE STABBED IN THE FACE AND SET FIRE TO.

HE COMES BACK IN THE MORNING TO SAY SORRY, BUT WHEN HE GETS INTO THE HOUSE THERE'S ONLY A DOG TIED TO THE BED. ODIN'S FUCKING FURIOUS, BUT HE REALLY SHOULD HAVE JUST LISTENED THE FIRST TIME SHE TOLD HIM TO FUCK OFF. ODIN'S A FUCKING DICK.

MOTHERFUCKING CRAZY MURDER-DWARVES

ONE OF THE FIRST MEN THE GODS MAKE IS KVASIR. HE'S A FUCKING WIZARD, AND HE KNOWS EVERYTHING. LITERALLY FUCKING EVERYTHING. ONE DAY, HE GOES FOR A WALK IN THE WOODS, AND A PAIR OF INSANE DWARVES (FJALAR AND GJALLAR) JUMP OUT OF A BUSH WITH AXES AND MURDER HIM TO DEATH. IT'S FUCKING HORRIFIC.

FJALAR AND GALAR MIX KVASIR'S BLOOD WITH HONEY, AND FERMENT IT INTO MAGICAL WIZARD MEAD. THE MAGICAL WIZARD MEAD GIVES ANYONE THAT DRINKS IT THE ABILITY TO WRITE FUCKING AMAZING POETRY, SO NATURALLY THE DWARVES BOTTLE IT UP AND SIT ON IT, BECAUSE DWARVES ARE EVIL LITTLE SHITS.

NEXT, THEY INVITE A GIANT CALLED GILLING AND HIS WIFE (WHO DOESN'T EVEN HAVE A FUCKING NAME) OVER FOR DINNER. THEY TAKE GILLING OUT FISHING FIRST, PUSH HIM OVERBOARD AND DROWN HIM. THEY DON'T EVEN HAVE A REASON FOR THIS, THEY'RE JUST COMPLETELY FUCKING INSANE AND LIKE TO MURDER PEOPLE. WHAT A BUNCH OF DICKS.

FJALLAR TELLS GILLING'S WIFE WHAT HAPPENED, AND OFFERS TO SHOW HER WHERE HER FUCKING HUSBAND DIED. AS SOON AS SHE LEAVES THE HOUSE, THOUGH, GALLAR DROPS A FUCKING MASSIVE MILLSTONE ON HER FUCKING HEAD, AND SHE DIES. DWARVES ARE ALL AWFUL PEOPLE.

UNFORTUNATELY THEY FORGOT ABOUT GILLING'S SON SUTTUNGR, WHO SHOWS UP AT THEIR HOUSE AND THREATENS TO BEAT THE SHIT OUT OF THEM AND DROWN THEM. FORTUNATELY FOR FJALLAR AND GJALLAR, GIANTS ARE FUCKING EASY TO BRIBE AND DON'T REALLY GIVE A SHIT ABOUT FAMILY. THEY OFFER HIM THE MAGICAL WIZARD MEAD, AND HE HAPPILY FUCKS OFF.

RETURN OF THE MAGICAL WIZARD MEAD

EVENTUALLY ODIN FINDS OUT ABOUT SUTTUNG AND HIS MAGICAL WIZARD MEAD, AND HE DECIDES HE WANTS IT. ODIN LIKES TO BE GOOD AT THINGS, AND HE'S AN EXPERT AT COMPLETELY FUCKING INSANE PLANS.

HE SETS OFF TO SUTTUNG'S HOUSE, AND ON THE WAY HE MEETS SOME FARMERS WHO REALLY WANT TO BUY HIS WHETSTONE. HE JUST LOBS IT UP IN THE AIR AND LETS THEM FUCKING MURDER EACH OTHER FOR IT. WHEN THEY'RE ALL DEAD HE PICKS IT UP AGAIN AND CONTINUES ON HIS WAY. ODIN REALLY IS A FUCKING DICK.

ODIN IS A DICK, AND HE'S ALSO ONE HELL OF A LAZY MOTHERFUCKER. HE STAYS AT THE HOUSE OF SUTTUNG'S BROTHER BAUGI, WHO WANTS HIS FAIR SHARE OF THE WIZARD MEAD. HE GIVES BAUGI A FUCKING MASSIVE DRILL, AND TELLS HIM TO BURROW INTO SUTTUNG'S MOUNTAIN. WHEN THERE'S A TINY HOLE, ODIN TURNS INTO A SNAKE AND SNEAKS IN.

IN ORDER TO GET AT THE MEAD, THOUGH, HE HAS TO GET PAST SUTTUNG'S DAUGHTER GUNNLOD. ODIN BEING A HORNY MOTHERFUCKER, HE JUST FUCKS HER FOR THREE WHOLE NIGHTS. THIS ENTITLES HIM TO THREE DRINKS OF THE MEAD, BUT HE JUST STEALS THE WHOLE BOTTLE AND FUCKS OFF.

HE DOESN'T EVEN CALL HER IN THE MORNING.

ELFNAPPING IS A BAD IDEA

VOLUNDR IS THE KING OF THE NORSE ELVES, AND HE'S FUCKING MISERABLE. HERVOR-ALVITR, HIS VALKYRIE WIFE, HAS JUST LEFT HIM, SO HE'S SITTING ON A TREE STUMP CRYING LIKE A WHINY LITTLE BITCH. MOTHERFUCKING ELVES.

WHILE VOLUNDR IS MOPING ABOUT, NIÐUÐR, THE KING OF SWEDEN, THROWS A BAG OVER HIS HEAD AND WHISKS HIM OFF BACK TO SWEDEN. WHAT A DICK.

VOLUNDR WAKES UP IN THE MORNING TO FIND THAT NIÐUÐR HAS CUT HIS LEGS OFF AND PUT HIM NEXT TO A FORGE. HE SPENDS A WEEK MAKING JEWELLERY FOR NIÐUÐR BEFORE HE GETS BORED AND DECIDES HE'S HAD ENOUGH OF THIS SHIT.

THEN HE MURDERS NIÐUÐR AND BOTH HIS SONS, FUCKS HIS DAUGHTER AND FLIES OFF INTO THE SUNSET LAUGHING LIKE A FUCKING MANIAC BECAUSE *WHO NEEDS LEGS ANYWAY.*

THOR THE OVERPROTECTIVE DAD

THOR HAS A TEENAGE DAUGHTER CALLED ÞRUÐR. (IN CASE YOU MOTHERFUCKERS WERE WONDERING, THAT BASICALLY TRANSLITERATES TO THRUTHR). THOR LOVES ÞRUÐR TO BITS, AND IS MORE THAN PREPARED TO BEAT THE SHIT OUT OF ANY BOYFRIEND SHE MAY EVER HAVE. EVEN IF THE BOYFRIEND IS A PRETTY GREAT DUDE, THOR HAS A FUCKING MASSIVE HAMMER AND LIKES BEATING THE SHIT OUT OF PEOPLE.

ONE DAY, ÞRUÐR GETS A BOYFRIEND CALLED ALVISS. (NO, NOT ELVIS. ALTHOUGH IF YOU IMAGINE ALVISS AS HAVING THE HAIR AND THE TROUSERS THEN THE WHOLE STORY GETS EVEN MORE FUCKING RIDICULOUS). ALVISS IS A DWARF, AND THOR REALLY FUCKING HATES DWARVES. UNFORTUNATELY FOR THOR AND HIS PROPENSITY FOR BEATING THE SHIT OUT OF DWARVES WITH A HAMMER, ÞRUÐR ASKS HIM NOT TO HIT HER BOYFRIEND IN THE FACE.

THOR TELLS ALVISS THAT HE NEEDS TO BE TALLER IN ORDER TO DATE HIS DAUGHTER, AND ALVISS TELLS HIM TO FUCK OFF. AT THIS POINT, THOR HAS A CUNNING PLAN. OR AT LEAST, AS CLOSE TO A CUNNING PLAN AS THOR IS CAPABLE OF. THOR IS FUCKING SHIT AT PLANS THAT DON'T INVOLVE VIOLENCE OR **CROSS-DRESSING**. HE ASKS ALVISS TO NAME ALL OF THE SHIT IN THE WORLD IN EVERY SINGLE FUCKIING LANGUAGE IN THE ENTIRE WORLD, AND ALVISS AGREES, BECAUSE HE'S FUCKING STUPID AND ÞRUÐR IS FUCKING HOT. SHE'S PROBABLY GOT A BEARD JUST LIKE HER DAD'S AND EVERYTHING - JUST LIKE ANY SEXY-AS-FUCK DWARF, ONLY TALLER.
ALVISS NAMES THINGS ALL NIGHT LONG, AND THEN THE SUN COMES UP AND HE TURNS TO STONE. NOW HE'S DEAD, AND THOR DIDN'T EVEN HAVE TO SMACK HIM IN THE FACE WITH A FUCKING HAMMER. THOR IS ONE HELL OF AN OVERPROTECTIVE DAD, AND ÞRUÐR WILL PROBABLY NEVER GET A BOYFRIEND WHO LIVES LONGER THAN A FUCKING WEEK AFTER ASKING HER OUT.

END OF THE FUCKING NORSE WORLD

SOME DAY, HELPFULLY NOT FUCKING SPECIFIED IN NORSE MYTHOLOGY, BUT IT COULD BE THIS FUCKING YEAR, THERE WILL COME THE WINTER TO END ALL WINTERS. IT'S GOING TO BE PRETTY FUCKING SHIT. AFTER THREE SHITTY WINTERS IN A ROW (AND NO SUMMER) EVERYONE IS GOING TO FUCKING HATE EACH OTHER, RIOTING ON THE STREETS AND ALL THAT SHIT.

THEN TWO FUCKING MONSTRUOUS WOLVES WILL ROCK UP, ONE (SKOLL) WILL EAT THE SUN, HIS BROTHER HATI WILL EAT THE FUCKING MOON. THEN THE STARS WILL FUCK OFF. NEXT SOME CHICKENS START MAKING FUCKING CHICKEN NOISES, CALLING THE GIANTS AND THE GODS TO BATTLE. ONE OF THE CHICKENS WILL ALSO RAISE THE FUCKING DEAD.

THERE'S GOING TO BE A SHIT TONNE OF EARTHQUAKES, BUT DON'T WORRY, THAT'S JUST FUCKING FENRIR, LOKI'S SCARY ASS WOLF SON, BREAKING FREE FROM HIS CHAINS AND COMING TO FUCK SHIT UP AND EAT EVERYTHING. THE SEA IS ALSO GOING TO BE FUCKED UP. THAT'LL BE JORMUNGAND, THE MIDGARD SERPENT, ANOTHER OF LOKI'S FUCKED UP MENAGERIE OF CHILDREN. HE'LL SHOW UP TO FUCK SHIT UP AND EAT THINGS TOO.

THEN ALL THE DEMONS OF HELL, PLUS ALL THE GIANTS AND FIERY NASTIES WILL COME AND START DESTROYING EARTH. IT'S GOING TO BE FUCKING AWESOME. FINALLY THE GODS WILL GET THEIR SHIT TOGETHER AND CALL TOGETHER LITERALLY FUCKING EVERYONE IN SOME HUGE END-LEVEL FIGHT. THOR WILL FIGHT AND KILL FUCKING JORMUNGAND, BUT THE SNAKE'S POISON WILL KILL HIM SOON AFTER. HEIMDALL AND LOKI WILL KILL EACHOTHER, AND AFTER A LONG FIGHT FENRIR WILL EAT ODIN. IT'S A PRETTY AWFUL ENDING.

ALL OF THE FUCKING NINE WORLDS WILL BURN, AND THE EARTH WILL SINK INTO THE SEA AND CRAZY SHIT LIKE THAT.

BUT AFTER THAT THERE'S GOING TO BE THIS AWESOME NEW AGE, AND EVERYTHING WILL BE FUCKING GREAT. DON'T WORRY ABOUT THE APOCALYPSE, MOTHERFUCKERS. ALL WILL BE FINE.

AFRICAN MYTHOLOGY

BEGINNINGS: WEST AFRICAN STYLE

IN THE BEGINNING, ALL THERE IS IN THE WORLD ARE A BUNCH OF GODS THAT LIVE IN THE FUCKING SKY AND A HUGE SHITTY EMPTY MARSH BELOW. OLORUN, THE CHIEF GOD, IS HAPPY FUCKING ABOUT IN THE SKY, BUT HIS SON OBATALA THINKS EVERYTHING IS SHIT AND SETS OUT TO CREATE THE WORLD.

OBATALA CREATES A HUGE GOLD CHAIN, A PALM-NUT, A PILE OF SAND, A CHICKEN AND A CAT. IT'S A PRETTY FUCKING WEIRD LIST OF THINGS, BUT HE HAS A PLAN.

HE CLIMBS DOWN THE GOLD CHAIN TO THE WATER, MAKES AN ISLAND WITH THE SAND, PLANTS THE PALM-NUT, RELEASES THE CHICKEN, AND SETTLES DOWN TO LIVE ON HIS NEW ISLAND WITH HIS MOTHERFUCKING CAT. THE ISLAND'S ENTIRELY POPULATED BY CHICKENS, BUT IT'S GOOD ENOUGH, OBATALA HAS HIS CAT AND THAT'S ALL HE NEEDS TO BE FUCKING HAPPY.

THERE YOU GO, THE WORLD IS CREATED BY A CRAZY CAT DUDE. THIS EXPLAINS ONE FUCKING HELL OF A LOT ABOUT THE WORLD.

POPULATING THE EARTH

OBATALA LIVES HAPPILY ON HIS ISLAND WITH HIS CAT AND HIS FUCKING CHICKENS FOR A WHILE. THE OTHER GODS ASK HIM TO COME BACK UP TO THE SKY A FEW TIMES, BUT HE'S A STUBBORN MOTHERFUCKER SO HE REFUSES.

IN THE END, THOUGH, HE GETS LONELY. HE TALKS TO HIS CAT, BUT IT DOESN'T TALK BACK. CATS ARE SHIT FRIENDS. BORED AND LONELY, HE STARTS MAKING PEOPLE OUT OF CLAY. HE MAKES A SHITLOAD OF THEM, AND THEN REALISES HE'S BEEN OUT IN THE HOT SUN FOR FUCKING HOURS AND HE NEEDS A MOTHERFUCKING DRINK. HE MAKES A BATCH OF PALM WINE, AND DRINKS THE WHOLE FUCKING THING.

UNFORTUNATELY, BY THE TIME HE GETS BACK TO WORK, THE ALCOHOL HAS HIT AND HE'S COMPLETELY WASTED. HE MAKES ANOTHER SHITLOAD OF PEOPLE, BUT THEY'RE KIND OF SHITTY AND UNEVEN BECAUSE HE'S FUCKING DRUNK AND HIS HANDS ARE CLUMSY.

HE BRINGS THEM ALL TO LIFE AND THEN HAS A NAP. WHEN HE WAKES UP, HE'S GOT A BITCH OF A HANGOVER, AND HE REALISES WHAT HE'S DONE.

HE FEELS LIKE SHIT FOR MAKING A BUNCH OF PEOPLE THAT DON'T MATCH THE REST, SO HE VOWS NEVER TO DRINK AGAIN AND BECOMES THE OFFICIAL PROTECTOR OF DISABLED PEOPLE, BECAUSE HE'S AN OK GUY REALLY, EVEN THOUGH HE FUCKED UP.

BABY SKY GODS

NANA BAKALU, THE MOTHER GODDESS, HAS ONE CHILD BEFORE RETIRING. SHE'S A PRETTY FUCKING LAZY MOTHER GODDESS. THE CHILD IS ANDROGYNOUS, AND HAS TWO FUCKING HEADS. THERE'S A MALE HEAD, CALLED LISA, WITH THE SUN FOR EYES, AND A FEMALE HEAD, CALLED MAWU, WITH THE MOON FOR EYES. MAWU-LISA IS PRETTY FUCKING AWESOME.

MAWU-LISA HAS SEVEN CHILDREN. THE FIRST TWO ARE TWINS CALLED DA ZODJI AND NYOHWE ANANU. THEN THERE'S ANOTHER FUCKING TWO HEADED ANDROGYNOUS BABY, WHO'S CALLED SOGBO. THEN TWO MORE TWINS, AGBE AND NAETE. THEN TWO NON-TWINS CALLED AGE AND GU. AGE IS A NORMAL FUCKING BABY, BUT GU IS MADE OF STONE. ASO HE DOESN'T HAVE A HEAD. HE JUST HAS A MOTHERFUCKING SWORD COMING OUT OF HIS NECK. IT'S PRETTY FUCKED-UP. THE SIXTH CHILD IS A FUCKING CLOUD, NOT A BABY, AND IS CALLED DJO, AND THE SEVENTH IS ANOTHER NORMAL BABY CALLED LEGBA. THEY'RE A PRETTY FUCKING WEIRD FAMILY.

DA ZODJI AND HYOHWE ANANU ARE PUT IN CHARGE OF THE FUCKING EARTH. SOGBO GETS THE SKY. AGBE AND NAETE GET THE SEA, AND AGE GETS THE ANIMALS. GU GETS ALL THE FARMS AND THE FORESTS, BECAUSE OBVIOUSLY A MUTANT SWORD-BABY IS GOING TO BE A FUCKING AMAZING FARMER. DJO GETS THE GAP BETWEEN THE EARTH AND THE SKY, BECAUSE HE'S A MOTHERFUCKING CLOUD, AND LEGBA DOESN'T GET A PROPER JOB BECAUSE HE'S A FUCKING BABY AND BABIES ARE SHIT WITH RESPONSIBILITY.

DEATH IS AN ANGRY GIANT

ONE DAY, A YOUNG MAN GOES OUT HUNTING TO FEED HIS FAMILY. INSTEAD OF FINDING FOOD, THOUGH, HE FINDS A MOTHERFUCKING GIANT. THE GIANT TELLS HIM ITS NAME IS OWUO, BUT HE CAN CALL IT DEATH, AND OFFERS HIM A JOB.

THE YOUNG MAN WORKS FOR DEATH FOR WEEKS, CARRYING SHIT AROUND FOR IT AND GETTING FOOD IN RETURN. AFTER A FEW WEEKS, THOUGH, HE'S REALLY FUCKING HOMESICK AND ASKS FOR PERMISSION TO GO HOME. DEATH AGREES, ON CONDITION THAT HE SENDS ANOTHER SERVANT IN HIS PLACE.

THE YOUNG MAN FUCKS OFF BACK HOME, AND SENDS HIS BROTHER OUT TO WORK FOR DEATH. AFTER A WHILE, THOUGH, HE DECIDES HE WANTS HIS JOB BACK AND GOES TO BOTHER DEATH AGAIN. DEATH GIVES HIM HIS JOB BACK, BECAUSE HIS BROTHER IS "ON A MOTHERFUCKING BUSINESS TRIP" AND WON'T BE BACK FOR A WHILE.

ONCE AGAIN, THOUGH, HE GETS HOMESICK. HE'S A STUPID INCONSISTENT MOTHERFUCKER. THE GIANT TELLS HIM TO FUCK OFF HOME AND SEND ANOTHER REPLACEMENT, AND HE DOES, SENDING HIS FUCKING SISTER TO WORK FOR DEATH.

YET AGAIN, HE DECIDES HE WANTS HIS JOB BACK AND GOES TO BOTHER DEATH. BECAUSE HIS SISTER IS "AWAY ON BUSINESS", DEATH GIVES HIM HIS JOB BACK AND OFFERS HIM DINNER AGAIN. THE YOUNG MAN IS PRETTY FUCKING PLEASED, AND SITS DOWN FOR DINNER.

HALF WAY THROUGH THE MAIN COURSE, HE SUDDENLY REALISES THAT THE BONES OF THE MEAT ARE MOTHERFUCKING HUMAN BONES. HE'S JUST EATEN HIS OWN FUCKING SISTER. FUCKING WHOOPS.

HE RUNS BACK TO THE VILLAGE IN A PANIC, AND ROUNDS UP AN ANGRY MOB TO BEAT THE SHIT OUT OF DEATH. THEY SNEAK UP ON DEATH WHILE IT'S ASLEEP, AND SET FIRE TO ITS FUCKING

HAIR. DEATH RUNS AROUND SCREAMING FOR A BIT, BECAUSE ITS HAIR IS ON FUCKING FIRE. FUNNILY ENOUGH, THIS MAKES DEATH PRETTY FUCKING FURIOUS, AND HE STARTS KILLING PEOPLE. AND THAT'S HOW MOTHERFUCKING DEATH WORKS.

AFRICAN SPIDER-MAN

SOMEWHERE IN WEST AFRICA THERE'S A KINGDOM WITH A SPECIAL SHEEP. THE KING FUCKING LOVES THIS SHEEP. THE KING PROBABLY FUCKS THE SHEEP TOO. WHY ELSE WOULD HE CARE ABOUT IT SO MUCH?

ONE DAY, THE SPECIAL SHEEP WANDERS ON TO THE LAND OF ANANSI THE FARMER. ANANSI IS FUCKING FURIOUS, BECAUSE THE SHEEP IS EATING HIS CROPS. SHEEP ARE DICKS. ANANSI THROWS A ROCK AT THE SHEEP'S HEAD, INTENDING TO SCARE IT OFF. UNFORTUNATELY, HE FUCKS UP. HE FUCKS UP REALLY BADLY, AND ACCIDENTALLY KILLS THE SHEEP. SHIT.

ANANSI PANICS, BECAUSE HE KNOWS THE KING IS GOING TO BE FUCKING FURIOUS THAT HIS FAVOURITE SHEEP IS DEAD. BUT THEN HE HAS A CUNNING PLAN. ANANSI IS FUCKING GREAT AT CUNNING PLANS. HE GRABS A BUNCH OF NUTS FROM THE NEAREST TREE AND HIDES THE FUCKING DEAD SHEEP UP THE TREE, SCARING THE SHIT OUT OF ALL THE NEARBY BIRDS AND SEVERELY TRAUMATISING THEIR BABIES FOR LIFE. ANANSI'S A BIT OF A DICK, BUT HE'S A DEVIOUS LITTLE SHIT.

ANANSI VISITS HIS FRIEND KUSUMBULI AND FEEDS HIM THE NUTS. KUSUMBULI IS FUCKING EXCITED, BECAUSE HE FUCKING LOVES NUTS. ANANSI LEADS HIM TO THE TREE TO GET MORE, AND TELLS HIM TO SHAKE THE FUCKING TREE TO MAKE THE NUTS FALL OUT. KUSUMBULI SHAKES THE TREE, BUT NO NUTS FALL OUT. INSTEAD HE GETS A MOTHERFUCKING DEAD SHEEP.

ANANSI BLAMES KUSUMBULI FOR THE FACT THAT THE SHEEP IS FUCKING DEAD, AND TURNS HIM IN TO THE POLICE. THE KING ISN'T THAT FUCKING STUPID, THOUGH, AND KNOWS THAT SHEEP ARE FUCKING SHIT AT CLIMBING TREES. THE KING CONCLUDES THAT ANANSI KILLED THE SHEEP, AND KICKS THE SHIT OUT OF HIM SO HARD THAT HE TURNS INTO A MOTHERFUCKING SPIDER.

ANANSI KIDNAPS EVERYONE

ANANSI, THE DEVIOUS SPIDER, WANTS TO BUY A BUNCH OF STORIES FROM NYAME, THE SKY GOD. THE SKY GOD IS A CRAZY MOTHERFUCKER, THOUGH, AND HIS PRICE IS FUCKING RIDICULOUS. HE WANTS THE BIGGEST PYTHON IN THE AREA, ALL THE ANGRY BEES, AND THE FASTEST LEOPARD. HIS MOTIVES FOR THIS ARE UNKNOWN AND PROBABLY SINISTER AS FUCK.

ANANSI HAPPILY ACCEPTS, AND SETS OUT TO ABDUCT ALL THE VICTIMS THE MOTHERFUCKING SKY GOD WANTS.

FIRST, HE GETS A FUCKING MASSIVE STICK AND SOME STRING, AND WALKS PAST THE PYTHON'S HOUSE LOUDLY SHOUTING ABOUT HOW SHIT PYTHONS ARE AND HOW MUCH BETTER HIS STICK IS THAN A FUCKING SNAKE. THIS SOUNDS LIKE A EUPHEMISM BUT ACTUALLY IT'S A FUCKING CUNNING PLAN. THE PYTHON COMES OUT OF HIS HOUSE AND LIES DOWN NEXT TO THE STICK TO PROVE THAT HE'S LONGER, AND ANANSI TIES HIM TO THE STICK AND FUCKS OFF.

THEN HE SETS OUT TO STEAL ALL THE FUCKING ANGRY BEES. HE GETS A BOX AND A BUCKET OF WATER, THROWS THE WATER OVER THE BEES' NEST, AND SHOUTS ABOUT HOW EVERYTHING IS ABOUT TO FLOOD. THE BEES FREAK THE FUCK OUT, AND ALL HIDE IN HIS BOX TO STAY DRY. ANANSI CLOSES THE BOX AND PUTS THE ANGRY BEES IN HIS PILE OF FUCKING KIDNAP VICTIMS.

THE LEOPARD IS EASIER. ANANSI JUST DIGS A FUCKING MASSIVE HOLE IN THE GROUND, AND WAITS FOR THE LEOPARD TO FALL INTO IT. LEOPARDS ARE FUCKING STUPID. HE TIES THE LEOPARD UP TOO, AND HANDS OVER ALL HIS VICTIMS TO THE SKY GOD FOR WHATEVER DEPRAVED NEFARIOUS FUCKERY HE WANTS THEM FOR.

ANANSI GETS THE STORIES HE WANTS, AND IS FREE TO SPEND THE REST OF HIS LIFE FUCKING ABOUT AND MAKING LIFE FUCKING SHIT FOR EVERYONE ELSE, SO HE'S HAPPY.

ANANSI HAGGLES LIKE A MEAN MOTHERFUCKER

NOBODY LIKES ANANSI, BECAUSE NOT ONLY IS HE A SPIDER, HE'S ALSO A MOTHERFUCKING CHEAT. DETERMINED TO FIX THIS, HE TRIES TO SNEAK IN TO WULBARI (THE SKY GOD)'S GOOD BOOKS. ANANSI COMES UP TO WULBARI AND ASKS IF HE CAN BORROW A CORN COB. HE SAYS THAT IN RETURN HE'LL GIVE WULBARI A HUNDRED FUCKING SLAVES. WULBARI THINKS THIS IS SO FUCKING STUPID THAT IT'S JUST HILARIOUS, AND GIVES HIM THE CORN.

ANANSI TAKES HIS CORN COB AND GOES TO STAY IN A VILLAGE SOMEWHERE. WHEN EVERYONE'S ASLEEP, HE EATS THE CORN AND BLAMES THE CHIEF FOR IT. EVERYONE IN THE VILLAGE IS SO FUCKING EMBARRASSED THAT THEY PAY HIM OFF WITH A WHOLE BASKET OF CORN EACH. ANANSI LOADS ALL THE CORN INTO A SACK AND FUCKS OFF.

ON THE WAY TO THE NEXT VILLAGE, HE MANAGES TO SWAP THE CORN FOR A CHICKEN. WHEN HE GETS TO THE VILLAGE, HE STABS THE CHICKEN IN THE FACE AND THEN RUBS THE BLOOD ALL OVER THE CHIEF WHILE HE'S ASLEEP. THIS TIME, THE VILLAGERS ARE SO ASHAMED OF THEIR BRUTAL CHICKEN-MURDERING CHIEF THAT THEY EACH GIVE ANANSI A WHOLE FUCKING SHEEP.

ON HIS WAY TO THE THIRD VILLAGE, ANANSI SPOTS A BUNCH OF PEOPLE CARRYING A CORPSE. HE OFFERS THEM ALL HIS SHEEP FOR THE CORPSE, AND BECAUSE DEAD PEOPLE ARE FUCKING USELESS AND PRESUMABLY THEY DIDN'T LIKE THE POOR DUDE VERY MUCH (ALSO HE WAS BEGINNING TO SMELL A BIT) THEY ACCEPT.

ANANSI REACHES THE LAST VILLAGE IN THE AREA, CLAIMS THE CORPSE IS THE SON OF WULBARI, AND THAT HE'S JUST TIRED AND IN NEED OF A BED. ALSO THAT HE HASN'T HAD A FUCKING BATH IN WEEKS. IN THE MORNING, HE TELLS THE KIDS OF THE VILLAGE TO GO AND HIT THE BODY WITH STICKS TO WAKE IT

UP, AND THEN CLAIMS THEY'VE BEATEN WULBARI'S FAVOURITE SON TO DEATH. ANANSI IS A LYING LITTLE SHIT. IN PENANCE FOR BEATING THE SHIT OUT OF THE CORPSE, THE VILLAGERS GIVE ANANSI A HUNDRED CHILDREN TO GO TO WULBARI WITH HIM AND SAY SORRY. ANANSI TAKES THE CHILDREN, FUCKS OFF, GIVES THEM TO WULBARI AS SLAVES, AND IS NEVER SEEN AGAIN BY THE POOR VILLAGERS. WHAT A FUCKING DICK.

FIRE IS A SHIT FRIEND

LEOPARD IS BEST FRIENDS WITH FIRE. THEY HAVE A SAD AND FUCKED-UP FRIENDSHIP, WHERE LEOPARD GOES TO VISIT FIRE EVERY DAY BUT FIRE NEVER COMES TO VISIT LEOPARD.

LEOPARD'S WIFE DOESN'T BELIEVE HE ACTUALLY HAS ANY FRIENDS, SO SHE TAKES THE PISS OUT OF HIM MERCILESSLY FOR PRETENDING TO HAVE A FRIEND CALLED FIRE. IN THE END, LEOPARD CAN'T TAKE HER BITCHING ANY MORE, AND ASKS FIRE OVER FOR DINNER. FIRE TELLS HIM TO FUCK OFF, BUT HE KEEPS NAGGING UNTIL FIRE AGREES TO COME ROUND.

LEOPARD GETS EVERYTHING READY, CLEANS THE HOUSE, AND MAKES A FUCKING BEAUTIFUL DINNER. HE'S GETTING REALLY EXCITED, BUT WHEN FIRE COMES IN THROUGH THE FRONT DOOR THE ENTIRE MOTHERFUCKING HOUSE BURNS DOWN AND LEOPARD AND HIS WIFE HAVE TO DIVE OUT OF THE WINDOW AND INTO THE RIVER. NOW THEY'RE COVERED IN BLACK BURN MARKS AND SOAKING WET, AND THEIR HOUSE HAS JUST BURNED TO THE GROUND. EVERYTHING IS FUCKING SHIT.

TORTOISES ARE SHIT AT CLIMBING TREES

WHEN THE BABOON GETS MARRIED, HE INVITES HIS BEST FRIEND THE TORTOISE. UNFORTUNATELY FOR THE POOR TORTOISE, THE WEDDING HAPPENS AT THE TOP OF A TREE. TORTOISES ARE FUCKING SHIT AT CLIMBING TREES, SO EVERY TIME HE TRIES TO TAKE A BITE OF ANY OF THE FOOD HE FALLS OFF HIS BRANCH AND HAS TO CLIMB UP IT AGAIN. IT'S FUCKING EMBARRASSING.

THE TORTOISE VOWS REVENGE, SO WHEN HE GETS MARRIED HE BURNS ALL THE GRASS AROUND THE AREA, LEAVING FUCKLOADS OF BLACK ASH. WHEN THE BABOON ARRIVES AND SITS DOWN, HE GETS ASH ALL OVER HIS HANDS AND THE TORTOISE TELLS HIM HE'S BEING REALLY FUCKING RUDE AND SENDS HIM ALL THE WAY TO THE FUCKING RIVER TO WASH THAT SHIT OFF HIS HANDS. BY THE TIME THE BABOON GETS BACK, HALF THE FOOD HAS GONE. WHEN HE SITS DOWN AGAIN, HE GETS MORE OF THE FUCKING ASH ON HIS HANDS AND THE TORTOISE TELLS HIM TO STOP BEING SUCH A DICK AND CLEAN HIS HANDS PROPERLY THIS TIME.

THIS HAPPENS FIVE TIMES, AND BY THE END THERE'S NO FOOD LEFT AND THE BABOON IS FUCKING STARVING. TORTOISES ARE FUCKING DICKS. DON'T PROVOKE THEM.

CENTRAL AND SOUTH
AMERICAN MYTHOLOGY

BEGINNINGS: AZTEC STYLE

THE UNIVERSE STARTS OUT WITH JUST ONE GOD EXISTING. OMETECHUTLI, THE FIRST GOD (AND ALSO GODDESS. HE/SHE IS BOTH AT THE SAME TIME) MAKES FOUR MORE GODS AND THEN FUCKS OFF AND DOES NOTHING ELSE EVER AGAIN. HE/SHE IS REALLY PRETTY FUCKING USELESS.

THE FOUR USEFUL GODS ARE QUETZALCOATL, WHO'S THE CHIEF GOD AND CAN TURN INTO A GIANT FLYING SNAKE (THAT'S RIGHT, HE'S A MOTHERFUCKING DRAGON), HUITZILOPOCHTLI, THE GOD OF WAR, HUMAN SACRIFICE, AND SETTING SHIT ON FIRE, TEZCATLIPOCA, THE GOD OF NIGHT, OBSIDIAN, CHAOS AND MOTHERFUCKING JAGUARS, AND FINALLY XIPE TOTEC, THE GOD OF FARMING, WHO WEARS A HUMAN SKIN AS CLOTHES FOR NO REASON OTHER THAN THAT HE'S A DICK.

THEY MAKE A BUNCH MORE GODS AND SOME WATER AND ALSO A FUCKING MASSIVE CROCODILE SHARK MONSTER CALLED CIPACTLI. THAT WAS A PRETTY FUCKING STUPID IDEA, BECAUSE EVERY TIME THEY MAKE SOMETHING ELSE AFTER THAT, IT FALLS INTO THE WATER AND GETS EATEN BY AN ANGRY CROCODILE MONSTER. IN THE END THE GODS HAVE HAD ENOUGH, AND JUST TEAR CIPACTLI INTO PIECES. LITERALLY. WITH THEIR BARE HANDS.

THEN THE UNIVERSE IS MAGICALLY MADE OUT OF CHUNKS OF DEAD MONSTER. THE HEAD BECOMES THE SKY, THE BODY THE EARTH, AND THE TAIL FUCKS OFF DOWN INTO THE UNDERWORLD.

MAKING SUNS IS FUCKING DIFFICULT

WHEN THE WORLD HAS BEEN CREATED, THE GODS LOOK AT WHAT THEY'VE DONE AND THEN REALISE THAT THEY CAN'T BECAUSE IT'S ALL DARK. THEY'VE FORGOTTEN TO MAKE THE SUN. FUCKING WHOOPS.

HOW DO YOU MAKE A SUN? THAT'S RIGHT, YOU SACRIFICE A MOTHERFUCKING GOD. TEZCATLIPOCA GETS SACRIFICED, BUT THEY FUCK IT UP AND HE ONLY MAKES HALF THE SUN. CLOSE ENOUGH, THINK ALL THE OTHER GODS, AND MAKE A BUNCH OF GIANTS TO LIVE UNDER THE BURNING CORPSE OF THEIR BROTHER. TEZCATLIPOCA IS PRETTY FUCKING FURIOUS, WHICH IS UNDERSTANDABLE GIVEN THAT HE'S JUST BEEN SACRIFICED, AND INVENTS THE JAGUAR. THEN ALL THE GIANTS GET EATEN BY JAGUARS.

QUETZALCOATL HAS HAD ENOUGH OF THIS BULLSHIT, AND TAKES OVER BEING THE SUN. THEN ALL THE OTHER GODS MAKE HUMANS, AND IT'S ALL OK FOR A BIT.

ONLY FOR A BIT THOUGH. PRETTY SOON THE HUMANS START GOING A BIT CORRUPT, SO TEZCATLIPOCA TURNS THEM ALL INTO MONKEYS. THAT'S NOT THE BEST WAY TO FIX PROBLEMS, BUT HE'S ALREADY TRIED THE EATEN-BY-JAGUARS METHOD. QUETZALCOATL THINKS THIS IS FUCKING RIDICULOUS, SENDS A HURRICANE TO BLOW THE MONKEYS AWAY.

THE NEXT SUN IS TLALOC, GOD OF RAIN, WHO THE FIRST FOUR GODS MAKE AND THEN SACRIFICE PRETTY QUICKLY. UNFORTUNATELY, WHILE HE'S AWAY, TEZCATLIPOCA STEALS HIS WIFE. AS MENTIONED EARLIER, TEZCATLIPOCA IS A DICK. TLALOC REFUSES TO SEND ANY RAIN, AND THE EARTH DRIES UP. IN THE END TEZCATLIPOCA HAS HAD ENOUGH, AND, BECAUSE HE'S GREAT AT FIXING PROBLEMS, MAKES IT RAIN FIRE UNTIL THE EARTH IS DESTROYED. HE COULD HAVE JUST GIVEN TLALOC'S WIFE BACK, BUT WHERE WOULD THE FUN IN THAT BE?

THE NEXT SUN IS TLATLOC'S SISTER CALCHIUHTLICUE, AND SHE'S FUCKING GREAT. QUETZALCOATL AND TEZCATLIPOCA, HOWEVER, ARE JEALOUS, SO THEY THROW SHIT AT HER TILL SHE FALLS OUT OF THE SKY AND DESTROYS THE WORLD. AGAIN.

IN THE END THE GODS DECIDE THIS IS ALL FUCKING STUPID AND THEY AREN'T GETTING ANYWHERE, SO THEY THROW A BUNCH OF MINOR GODS AND ALSO A RABBIT AND AN EAGLE AND A JAGUAR INTO A FIRE AND MAKE THE SUN AND THE MOON, AND EVERYONE GETS TO LIVE HAPPILY EVER AFTER. EXCEPT THE MINOR GODS AND THE RABBIT AND THE EAGLE AND THE JAGUAR, BUT NOBODY GIVES A SHIT ABOUT THEM.

WHERE DO PEOPLE COME FROM?

SO NOW THE GODS HAVE MADE THE WORLD, BUT THEY HAVEN'T GOT ANY PEOPLE TO LIVE THERE. HOW DO YOU MAKE PEOPLE? FROM THE BONES OF ALL THE GIANTS AND JAGUARS AND MONKEYS THAT YOU'VE MURDERED BEFOREHAND, OF COURSE.

QUETZALCOATL GOES DOWN TO MICTLAN, THE UNDERWORLD, TO FETCH THE BONES. MICTLAN IS RULED BY MICTLANTECUHTLI, WHO'S BASICALLY A GIANT SKELETON SURROUNDED BY SPIDERS AND OWLS AND SPOOKY SHIT LIKE THAT. QUETZALCOATL ASKS IF HE CAN HAVE SOME MAGIC BONES, AND MICTLANTECUHTLI SAYS SURE, BUT ONLY IF HE DANCES ROUND HIS THRONE FOUR TIMES PLAYING THE TRUMPET.

QUETZALCOATL IS IMPOSSIBLE TO EMBARRASS, SO HE DOES A LITTLE DANCE AND PLAYS THE TRUMPET FOR A BIT. HOWEVER, HE DOESN'T TRUST MICTLANTECUHTLI, SO HE MAKES A MAGIC CLONE OF HIMSELF TO BE A DISTRACTION, STEALS THE BONES, AND FUCKS OFF. UNFORTUNATELY, MICTLAN IS FULL OF QUAIL FOR SOME FUCKING STUPID REASON, SO QUETZALCOATL TRIPS OVER A BIRD AND FALLS DOWN A HOLE ON THE WAY OUT, BREAKING THE BONES. THIS IS WHY PEOPLE COME IN DIFFERENT SIZES.

A GODLY PISS-UP

AFTER THE EARTH, THE SUN, AND PEOPLE HAVE BEEN CREATED, WHAT'S THE NEXT MOST IMPORTANT THING? THAT'S RIGHT, MOTHERFUCKERS. ALCOHOL.

ONE DAY MAYAHUEL (THE GODDESS OF SHITTY CACTI) SEES A MOUSE EATING ROTTING FRUIT AND GETTING DRUNK, AND THINKS THAT LOOKS LIKE FUN. SHE GATHERS UP A BUNCH OF FRUIT AND SEEDS, AND INVENTS A DRINK CALLED PULQUE, WHICH IS BASICALLY TEQUILA FOR GODS. IT GETS ALL THE GODS DRUNK AND MAKES THEM ALL HALLUCINATE SOME FUCKING WEIRD SHIT.

WHILE THEY'RE ALL DRUNK, THE GODS MAKE A BUNCH OF OTHER GODS. BUT THEY'RE DRUNK SO THE NEW GODS ARE REALLY SHITTY. AS A RESULT OF THIS, THE AZTEC GOD OF ALCOHOL IS A BIT UNUSUAL.

MOST MYTHOLOGIES FEATURE GODS OF ALCOHOL LIKE DIONYSUS; A BIT DISREPUTABLE BUT QUITE FUN. NOT THE AZTECS. HA HA FUCK NO. THE AZTEC GOD OF ALCOHOL IS... FOUR HUNDRED DRUNKEN RABBITS. NO, SERIOUSLY. FOUR HUNDRED MOTHERFUCKING RABBITS. DRUNK RABBITS.

QUETZALCOATL FUCKS UP

QUETZALCOATL IS THE CHIEF GOD, SO EVERYONE WORSHIPS HIM. THIS WOULD BE GREAT, ONLY HE "FORGETS" TO TELL THEM TO WORSHIP THE OTHER GODS TOO. SELFISH BASTARD.

TEZCATLIPOCA IS KIND OF JEALOUS, SO HE DECIDES TO FUCK SHIT UP FOR EVERYONE. HE SNEAKS DOWN TO EARTH, SPIKES QUETZALCOATL'S DRINK, AND SITS BACK TO WATCH THE CARNAGE. WHAT A DICK.

QUETZALCOATL GETS REALLY, REALLY DRUNK. WHEN A GOD GETS DRUNK, IT'S FUCKING INSANE. DRUNK AND CONFUSED, HE SLEEPS WITH HIS OWN SISTER. NEVER MIND WHICH MYTHOLOGY YOU LOOK AT, INCEST IS A FUCKING TERRIBLE IDEA.

HE WAKES UP IN THE MORNING WITH ONE HELL OF A HANGOVER, NEXT TO HIS SISTER, AND REALISES THAT HE'S FUCKED UP. HE'S FUCKED UP REALLY BADLY. JUST TO SHOW HOW SORRY HE IS, HE STABS HIMSELF THEN DIVES INTO A FIRE AND DIES. BEING AN AZTEC GOD, THOUGH, HE JUST COMES BACK TO LIFE.

GIVEN HE CAN'T KILL HIMSELF, HE DOES THE NEXT BEST THING: HE KNITS A RAFT OUT OF MOTHERFUCKING SNAKES AND SENDS HIMSELF INTO EXILE.

TEZCATLIPOCA IS A REALLY SHITTY WISH FAIRY

AS WE'VE ESTABLISHED BEFORE, TEZCATLIPOCA IS A DICK. HIS FAVOURITE ACTIVITY IS FUCKING AROUND WITH HUMANS AND FRIGHTENING THEM.

IN THE NIGHT, HE SNEAKS INTO PEOPLE'S BEDROOMS IN THE FORM OF A MOTHERFUCKING HEADLESS CORPSE AND GOES "BOO". HE'S ALSO GOT A GIANT GAPING WOUND IN HIS CHEST THAT FLAPS OPEN AND CLOSED AND MAKES A CREEPY NOISE. MOST PEOPLE, CONFRONTED BY A HEADLESS CORPSE WITH A FLAPPY CHEST HOLE, SCREAM THE AZTEC EQUIVALENT OF "FUCKING HELL" AND RUN AWAY AS FAST AS THEY FUCKING CAN.

IF THEY DO THAT THEN HE JUST EATS THEM, BECAUSE HE'S A DICK. IF THEY DON'T, THEN HE JUST STANDS THERE MAKING CREEPY NOISES. THE CORRECT ANSWER IN THIS CASE IS TO REACH INTO HIS CHEST AND TAKE OUT HIS HEART. IF HIS VICTIM DOES THIS THEN HE GIVES THEM A MAGIC WISH AND VANISHES IN A PUFF OF SHITTY FAIRY DUST.

IF THEY JUST STAND THERE AND ARE TOO FUCKING SQUEAMISH TO REACH INTO HIS FLAPPY CHEST HOLE, HE JUST EATS THEM ANYWAY. TEZCATLIPOCA REALLY IS A DICK.

BEWARE OF THE LLAMA

ONE DAY, A LLAMA FARMER IS FUCKING ABOUT IN A FIELD (SHH NO WELSH JOKES, HE'S AN INCA AND FUCKING LLAMAS IS PROBABLY FATAL), WHEN HE NOTICES THAT HIS FAVOURITE LLAMA IS IN TEARS. HE RUSHES TO CONSOLE THE POOR THING, AND IT TELLS HIM (IT'S A TALKING LLAMA. FUCK OFF). THAT IT'S SAD BECAUSE THE WORLD IS GOING TO FLOOD. THE FARMER PANICS AND DRAGS HIS FRIENDS AND FAMILY AND EVERY FUCKING ANIMAL HE CAN CATCH UP TO THE TOP OF THE HIGHEST MOUNTAIN, AND HE WAITS. SURE ENOUGH, IT STARTS RAINING AND THE ENTIRE FUCKING WORLD FLOODS. THE ONLY SURVIVORS ARE THOSE THAT MADE IT UP THE MOUNTAIN, AND THEY COUNT THEMSELVES REALLY FUCKING LUCKY TO HAVE MADE IT OUT ALIVE.

WHEN THE WATERS GO DOWN, THEY LEAVE THE MOUNTAIN, BUT IT'S NOT FUCKING OVER YET. SUDDENLY THE MOTHERFUCKING SUN GOES OUT. THE STONES COME TO LIFE AND WANDER ROUND THE FIELDS, AND THE LLAMAS TURN ON THEIR MASTERS. IT'S LIKE A SCENE FROM SOME SORT OF FUCKING INSANE HORROR MOVIE, WITH POOR INNOCENT FARMERS BEING TORN TO PIECES AND EATEN BY THEIR FLUFFY LLAMAS. THE LLAMA UPRISING GOES ON FOR FIVE DAYS, AND ALMOST EVERY SINGLE PERSON GETS EATEN. THE FIELDS ARE FLOODED WITH BLOOD, AND THE CRAZED MURDER-LLAMAS RAMPAGE ACROSS THE ANDES, LEAVING CHUNKS OF DEAD PERSON IN THEIR WAKE. DON'T TRUST A LLAMA. THOSE THINGS ARE FUCKING EVIL.

ANGRY GAY GIANTS

THE INCA LIVE HAPPILY IN PERU, FUCKING AROUND IN THE ANDES AND DOING ALL THE SHIT THEY DO. ONE DAY, THOUGH, A BUNCH OF MOTHERFUCKING GIANTS ARRIVE.

THEY SHOW UP IN FUCKING HUGE BOATS MADE OF REEDS. NOBODY HAS A FUCKING CLUE WHERE THEY CAME FROM, BUT THEY SEEM TO WANT TO STAY. THEY'RE ALL MALE, AND THEY ALL SPEND THEIR SPARE TIME FUCKING EACH OTHER. THE INCA WELCOME THEM, BUT THE GIANTS AREN'T HAVING ANY OF THAT SHIT. THEY EAT ALL THE ANIMALS AND PLANTS IN THE AREA, LEAVING THE INCA TO STARVE. GIANTS ARE FUCKING DICKS.

WHEN THE INCA TELL THE GIANTS TO FUCK OFF, THEY GET TURNED ON BY ANGRY MOTHERFUCKING GIANTS. ALL THE WOMEN GET EATEN, AND ALL THE MEN GET VIOLENTLY RAPED TO DEATH BY ANGRY GIANTS. IT'S A FUCKING MESS.

THE FEW SURVIVING INCA GO AND HIDE IN A CORNER, AND THE GIANTS GO BACK TO EATING THINGS AND FUCKING. FORTUNATELY THAT SHIT DOESN'T LAST LONG, BECAUSE THE INCAN GODS ARE ALL HOMOPHOBIC FUCKS. THEY'RE FINE WITH THE MAN-EATING AND MURDER, BUT ANY HINT OF ANAL SEX AND SHIT IS GOING TO GO DOWN. A BUNCH OF SPARKLY FUCKING ANGELS COME DOWN FROM THE SKY AND BURN ALL THE GIANTS TO DEATH. EVERYONE'S HAPPY, APART FROM THE PEOPLE THAT GOT EATEN OR RAPED TO DEATH. THIS SHIT'S PRETTY FUCKING DARK.

BEGINNINGS: MAYAN STYLE

IN THE BEGINNING THERE'S NOTHING BUT A BUNCH OF GODS. THE PROBLEM IS, DESPITE THE FACT THAT THE MAYA ARE STILL AROUND, NOBODY SEEMS TO HAVE A FUCKING CLUE WHO MOST OF THEIR GODS ARE. WHOEVER THEY ARE, THERE ARE SEVEN OF THEM, AND THEY MAKE THE EARTH AND THE SKY. THE GODS ARE PRETTY SHITTY BUILDERS, THOUGH, AND THE SKY FALLS DOWN. SURPRISE FLOOD, MOTHERFUCKERS!

IN THE END THE GODS MOP UP THE MESS, STICK THE SKY BACK UP, AND MAKE TREES TO HOLD IT UP PROPERLY THIS TIME.

NOW THEY'VE GOT A WORLD WHERE THE SKY DOESN'T FALL DOWN AND FUCK EVERYTHING UP ANY MORE, THE GODS MOVE ON TO MAKING PEOPLE. THEY START BY MAKING ANIMALS, BUT THAT'S NOT QUITE RIGHT, SO THEY START AGAIN. THE NEXT ATTEMPT INVOLVES MAKING PEOPLE OUT OF WET CLAY, BUT THE RESULTING PEOPLE ARE KIND OF RUNNY AND FUCKED UP. THEN THE GODS MOVE ON TO WOOD, BUT WOODEN PEOPLE DON'T FUCKING BEND. THE MAYAN GODS ARE PRETTY FUCKING STUPID. IN THE END THEY MAKE SOME SORT OF BREAD DOUGH OUT OF MAIZE, AND THE PEOPLE THEY MAKE OUT OF THAT ARE NORMAL PEOPLE THAT CAN TALK AND DO SHIT LIKE THAT. DESPITE FUCKING UP EVERYTHING SO MANY TIMES, THE GODS ARE FINALLY HAPPY AND THE WORLD EXISTS. AT FUCKING LAST.

FOOTBALL WITH DEATH

THE MAYAN GODS ARE LAZY MOTHERFUCKERS, SO AFTER THEY'VE MADE PEOPLE THEY MAKE A COUPLE OF HEROES TO KEEP AN EYE ON THE PEOPLE AND MAKE SURE THEY DON'T FUCK UP TOO BADLY.

UNFORTUNATELY, THE HERO TWINS CAN'T STOP THE PLAGUE FROM HAPPENING. THERE'S DISEASE EVERYWHERE AND PEOPLE ARE DYING ALL THE TIME. THE GODS FUCKED UP AGAIN.

IN ORDER TO DEAL WITH HOW SHIT EVERYTHING IS, THE HERO TWINS GO DOWN TO THE UNDERWORLD TO BEAT THE SHIT OUT OF THE GOD OF DEATH. WHEN THEY GET THERE, THOUGH, THERE ARE TWO GODS OF DEATH. THEIR NAMES ARE ONE-DEATH AND SEVEN-DEATH. PRESUMABLY DEATHS TWO THROUGH SIX ARE A BIT EMBARRASSING AND ARE KEPT IN A CUPBOARD SOMEWHERE OR SOMETHING LIKE THAT.

ONE-DEATH AND SEVEN-DEATH SUMMON ALL THEIR PLAGUE GODS, AND THERE ARE FUCKLOADS OF THOSE. THE HERO TWINS ARE ALL READY TO BEAT THE SHIT OUT OF THEM AND STOP THE PLAGUE, BUT INSTEAD THE DEATH GODS TELL THEM THAT'S NOT HOW SHIT WORKS DOWN IN THE UNDERWORLD. IN THE UNDERWORLD THEY SETTLE ARGUMENTS BY PLAYING FUCKING FOOTBALL.

FORTUNATELY THE HERO TWINS ARE REALLY FUCKING GOOD AT FOOTBALL, SO THEY BEAT THE PLAGUE GODS AND THE DEATH GODS AGREE TO STOP PLAGUING THE EARTH WITH PLAGUE. EVERYONE LIVES HAPPILY EVER AFTER, ESPECIALLY THE HERO TWINS, WHO GET TO BRING FOOTBALL UP TO EARTH ON THEIR WAY BACK AND THEN GET MADE INTO SUN AND MOON GODS AS A REWARD.

NATIVE AMERICAN
MYTHOLOGY

BEGINNINGS: IROQUOIS STYLE

BEFORE THE WORLD EXISTS, EVERYTHING IS MOTHERFUCKING DARKNESS AND WATER, ONLY POPULATED BY FISH AND DUCKS. IT'S FUCKING SHIT, UNLESS YOU'RE A FISH OR A DUCK. ABOVE THE CLOUDS EVERYTHING IS RAINBOWS AND SPARKLES AND GODS, AND IT'S ALL FUCKING FANTASTIC, BUT THE GODS ARE SELFISH FUCKS AND WON'T SHARE THEIR SPARKLES.

THE GODDESS ATAHENSIC IS PREGNANT, SO HER FAMILY WRAP HER UP IN RAYS OF LIGHT AND PUT HER TO BED. UNFORTUNATELY, SHE'S TOO FUCKING HEAVY, AND SINKS THROUGH THE BED. SHE STARTS FALLING TOWARDS THE DARK WATER BELOW, AND ALL THE DUCKS START TO FREAK THE FUCK OUT.

THE WATER CREATURES REALISE THAT THE ONLY THING STRONG ENOUGH TO STOP ATAHENSIC FROM CRUSHING EVERYONE TO DEATH IS THE MUD AT THE BOTTOM OF THE FUCKING WATER, AND THE BEAVER DIVES DOWN TO GET SOME. UNFORTUNATELY HE'S A SHIT SWIMMER, AND HE DROWNS. THEN THE DUCK TRIES, AND HE DROWNS TOO. BEING A SHIT SWIMMER IS ONE HELL OF A BIG DISADVANTAGE IN A WORLD MADE OF WATER.

IN THE END, THE MUSKRAT FETCHES SOME MUD AND SPREADS IT ALL OVER THE BIGGEST TURTLE HE CAN FIND, AND THEN LEAVES THE TURTLE THERE TO HOLD UP THE GODDESS. IT'S NOT FOREVER THOUGH, SO IT'S NOT QUITE AS MUCH OF A DICK MOVE AS IT SOUNDS.

THE SUN IS A MOTHERFUCKING SEVERED HEAD

AFTER A FEW DAYS OF LYING ON THE BACK OF A GIANT TURTLE, IT'S TIME FOR ATAHENSIC TO GIVE BIRTH. SHE HAS TWO CHILDREN, AND CALLS THEM HAHGWEDIYU AND HAHGWEDETAH. HAHGWEDIYU IS SPARKLY AS FUCK AND GENERALLY A GOOD GUY, AND HAHGWEDETAH IS JUST A DICK, DEDICATED TO FUCKING EVERYTHING UP FOR EVERYONE ELSE.

UNFORTUNATELY, ATAHENSIC DIES AND EVERYTHING GOES DARK. IN ORDER TO FIX THIS, HAHGWEDIYU TEARS HIS DEAD MOTHER'S HEAD FROM HER FUCKING SHOULDERS AND THROWS IT UP IN THE AIR. YOU THOUGHT THE SUN WAS A GIANT BALL OF FIRE? FUCK NO. IT'S A SEVERED HEAD.

HAHGWEDETAH DECIDES TO FUCK SHIT UP AT THIS POINT, AND CREATES THE NIGHT. HIS BROTHER IS DETERMINED TO MAKE MORE LIGHT, BUT THERE AREN'T ANY OTHER HEADS LYING AROUND THAT HE CAN MAKE SUNS WITH. WHAT'S THE BEST HEAD SUBSTITUTE? BOOBS. HAHGWEDIYU'S GRASP OF ANATOMY IS PRETTY SHIT, BUT HE TEARS HIS DEAD MOTHER'S BOOBS OFF AND THROWS THEM UP INTO THE SKY TO MAKE THE MOON. THEN HE BURIES THE MANGLED REMAINS OF HIS MOTHER'S CORPSE AND USES THAT TO MAKE ANIMALS AND SHIT LIKE THAT. THEN HE BURIES HIS BROTHER IN A FUCKING MASSIVE PIT, JUST TO MAKE SURE HE CAN'T FUCK IT ALL UP AGAIN

ANIMALS ARE VINDICTIVE FUCKS

AFTER THE WORLD HAS BEEN AROUND FOR A FEW YEARS, PEOPLE DECIDE TO START EATING MEAT. THE ANIMALS ARE PRETTY FUCKING PISSED OFF ABOUT BEING HACKED INTO LUMPS AND EATEN, SO THEY DECIDE TO FUCK SHIT UP FOR HUMANITY IN REVENGE.

ALL THE BEARS GET TOGETHER TO MAKE EVIL BEAR PLOTS, AND END UP DECIDING TO SHOOT ALL THE PEOPLE. THE PROBLEM IS, BEARS ARE SHIT AT ARCHERY. ONE OF THEM GETS HOLD OF A BOW AND TRIES TO SHOOT A GUY, BUT HIS CLAWS GET TANGLED IN THE STRING AND HE FALLS OVER. IN THE END, THE BEARS DECIDE THAT ARCHERY WAS A FUCKING SHIT IDEA AND RESIGN THEMSELVES TO THEIR INEVITABLE, DELICIOUS FATE.

ALL THE DEER HAVE A SIMILAR MEETING, BUT THEY DON'T EVEN TRY ARCHERY. DEER HAVE HOOVES, SO THEY'RE JUST AS SHIT WITH BOWS AS BEARS ARE, BUT THEY AREN'T QUITE AS FUCKING STUPID AS BEARS. THE DEER DECIDE STRAIGHTFORWARDLY TO POISON ANYONE WHO KILLS A DEER WITHOUT ASKING, BECAUSE DEER ARE ALL DICKS.

SO NOW, EVERY TIME SOMEONE SHOOTS A DEER WITHOUT ASKING FIRST, THE MOTHERFUCKING DEER FAIRY SNEAKS INTO THEIR BEDROOM AND POISONS THEM. AND THAT'S WHY YOU SHOULD ALWAYS SAY PLEASE BEFORE YOU DO ANY MURDERING. JUST IN CASE YOU GET POISONED BY A FUCKING ANGRY FAIRY.

DEMIGODS KNOW WHAT AMERICA WANTS

THE ONE HOT WOMAN IN THE WHOLE WORLD IS LONELY AS FUCK. FORTUNATELY FOR HER, SHE'S HOT ENOUGH THAT ONE OF THE GODS COMES DOWN AND FALLS IN LOVE WITH HER. BEING A GOD, HE JUST FUCKS HER AND LEAVES, BUT THAT'S ALL YOU CAN HOPE FOR FROM A GOD REALLY.

NINE MONTHS LATER, SHE HAS FOUR DEMIGOD CHILDREN, EACH OF WHOM SET OFF TO DO GOOD THINGS FOR HUMANITY. THE ELDEST IS CALLED MICHABO, AND HE'S JUST GENERALLY A PRETTY FUCKING GREAT GUY. THE NEXT IS CHIBIABOS, AND HE TAKES CHARGE OF THE LAND OF THE DEAD AND ALL THE DEAD SHIT RELATING TO THAT. THE THIRD KID IS WABASSA, AND HE JUST FUCKS OFF AND TURNS INTO A RABBIT, BECAUSE HE'S FUCKING INSANE AND ALSO REALLY FUCKING LOVES BUNNIES. THE YOUNGEST IS CHOKANIPOK, AND HE'S A DICK. HE'S SO MUCH OF A DICK, IN FACT, THAT HIS BROTHERS (EXCEPT FOR WABASSA, BECAUSE HE'S A FUCKING RABBIT) HACK HIM UP INTO SHITLOADS OF FUCKING TINY PIECES, AND TURN THEM INTO FLINT. THEN THEY TEAR OUT HIS BOWELS AND TURN THEM INTO PLANTS. HYGIENE IS OF NO FUCKING CONCERN TO THESE GUYS.

THEN MICHABO MAKES FOUR SPIRITS TO PROVIDE EVERYTHING THAT HUMANITY MIGHT EVER NEED. NAMELY: RAIN, SUN, SNOW, AND MELONS. BECAUSE MELONS ARE JUST THAT FUCKING IMPORTANT. MELONS AND RABBITS ARE CLEARLY AMONG THE MOST FUCKING VITAL ITEMS FOR LIFE. EITHER THAT OR MICHABO AND HIS BROTHERS ARE ALL REALLY FUCKING STUPID.

MOOWIS THE SEXY SNOWMAN

A YOUNG MAN FALLS MADLY IN LOVE WITH THE HOTTEST GIRL IN THE ENTIRE ALGONQUIN TRIBE, BUT SHE TELLS HIM TO FUCK OFF. HE'S NOT FUCKING PLEASED ABOUT THIS, AND VOWS TO MAKE HER LIFE AS SHITTY AS POSSIBLE.

HE GOES OUT INTO THE SNOW AND BUILDS A SNOWMAN. IT'S A REALLY FUCKING SEXY SNOWMAN, AND HE CALLS IT MOOWIS. THEN HE BREATHES ON IT AND IT COMES TO LIFE. THE YOUNG MAN EXPLAINS HIS EVIL PLOT TO MOOWIS THE SEXY SNOWMAN, AND SENDS HIM BACK TO THE VILLAGE.

MOOWIS ARRIVES IN THE VILLAGE, AND THE GIRL IMMEDIATELY FALLS FOR HIM, BECAUSE HE'S JUST THAT FUCKING HOT. THE TWO OF THEM GET MARRIED AND HAVE A HAPPY WINTER TOGETHER, EVEN THOUGH HE KEEPS REFUSING TO COME INSIDE AND SIT BY THE FIRE BECAUSE HE'S A FUCKING SNOWMAN AND SHE'S TOO FUCKING STUPID TO NOTICE.

UNFORTUNATELY FOR HER, AS SOON AS THE SUN COMES OUT IN SPRING, MOOWIS THE SEXY SNOWMAN MELTS. SHE FINDS HIS CLOTHES LYING IN A PUDDLE ON THE FLOOR, AND THINKS HE'S JUST FUCKED OFF COMPLETELY NAKED AND ABANDONED HER FOR SOME OTHER WOMAN. SHE'S FUCKING HEARTBROKEN AND SETS OFF ON AN EPIC FUCKING QUEST TO GET HER SNOWMAN HUSBAND BACK. HE'S NOT COMING BACK, THOUGH, BECAUSE HE'S FUCKING MELTED. SHE SPENDS HER ENTIRE FUCKING LIFE WANDERING THE WILDERNESS LOOKING FOR HIM, AND EVENTUALLY DIES OF OLD AGE. AND THAT'S WHY YOU SHOULDN'T MARRY A SNOWMAN, NEVER MIND HOW FUCKING SEXY HE MAY BE.

STEALING A BABY BEAVER

NOPATSIS IS THE SON OF A CHIEF, AND HE LIVES IN A HUT WITH HIS BROTHER, AKAIYAN. ONE DAY NOPATSIS GOES OUT HUNTING AND COMES BACK WITH A WIFE. NO FOOD, JUST A FUCKING WIFE. AKAIYAN IS FUCKING CONFUSED, BUT HE ACCEPTS THAT HIS BROTHER FELL MADLY IN LOVE WITH A STRANGE WOMAN AND BROUGHT HER HOME. THE WIFE IS, OF COURSE, A FUCKING EVIL WITCH.

WHEN NOPATSIS GOES OUT, HIS WIFE BEATS THE SHIT OUT OF HERSELF AND BLAMES AKAIYAN FOR IT. NOPATSIS BELIEVES EVERY WORD SHE SAYS, BECAUSE HE'S A FUCKING IDIOT, AND ABANDONS HIS BROTHER ON AN ISLAND TO DIE.

FORTUNATELY FOR AKAIYAN, HE GETS TAKEN IN BY A FAMILY OF BEAVERS, WHO KEEP HIM WARM ALL WINTER, FEED HIM, AND TEACH HIM TO SMOKE. BEAVERS ARE DISREPUTABLE FUCKS, AND PROBABLY SPEND THEIR SPARE TIME LOITERING OUTSIDE VILLAGES WITH CANS OF SPRAY PAINT WRITING RUDE MESSAGES ON THE WALLS. THEY'RE BASICALLY A FUCKING GANG OF SCARY BEAVERS WITH KNIVES AND LITTLE BEAVERY HOODIES. WHAT THE FUCK.

WHEN HE COMES OUT OF THE BEAVER LODGE IN THE SPRING, PROBABLY WITH A BUNCH OF NEW TATTOOS, AKAIYAN SEES HIS BROTHER'S BOAT ON THE SHORE. WHAT A CRAZY FUCKING COINCIDENCE. HE RUNS STRAIGHT BACK TO THE BEAVERS AND SAYS HE NEEDS TO FUCK OFF, AND THE CHIEF BEAVER TELLS HIM TO TAKE ANY ITEM HE LIKES AS A SOUVENIR. AKAIYAN GRABS THE NEAREST BABY BEAVER, BECAUSE IT'S FUCKING ADORABLE, AND GETS THE FUCK OUT OF THERE BEFORE ANYONE CAN TELL HIM TO STOP BEING SUCH A DICK.

THEY GET BACK TO THE VILLAGE, BANISH THE WITCH AND INTRODUCE THE PEOPLE TO MAGIC BEAVER MEDICINE. THIS IS SOME SORT OF COMPLICATED BULLSHIT INVOLVING MEDICINAL HERBS AND SHIT LIKE THAT, BUT IT SEEMS TO WORK REALLY

FUCKING WELL THEN THEY GO BACK TO THE ISLAND TO RESCUE NOPATSIS. UNFORTUNATELY, ALL THAT'S LEFT BY THE TIME AKAIYAN GETS THERE IS A PILE OF BONES. THE BEAVERS PROBABLY ATE HIM. BEAVERS ARE FUCKED UP.

GETTING REVENGE ON THE SUN

ONE DAY, A KID FALLS ASLEEP IN THE SUN, AND HIS FANCY AS FUCK COAT CATCHES FIRE IN THE HEAT. THE KID'S A LITTLE SHIT, AND VOWS REVENGE AGAINST THE SUN FOR RUINING HIS FUCKING FAVOURITE COAT.

HE MAKES HIMSELF A FUCKING MASSIVE NET OUT OF HIS SISTER'S HAIR, AND GETS UP IN THE MIDDLE OF THE NIGHT TO WAIT FOR THE SUN. WHEN THE SUN BEGINS TO RISE, THE KID THROWS HIS NET OVER IT AND TIES IT TO THE FLOOR.

AS A RESULT OF THE LITTLE SHIT'S INSISTENCE ON BLAMING THE SUN FOR HIS OWN FUCKING STUPIDITY, THERE'S NO LIGHT. ALL THE ANIMALS WAKE UP TO FIND IT'S STILL FUCKING DARK, AND PANIC.

EVENTUALLY THEY REALISE THAT THE SUN'S BEEN TIED DOWN, AND SOMEONE NEEDS TO CUT THROUGH THE NET. THE PROBLEM IS THAT THE SUN IS A FUCKING MASSIVE FIREBALL, AND ANYONE THAT GETS THAT CLOSE WILL PROBABLY CATCH FIRE AND BURN TO DEATH.

THE DORMOUSE IS FUCKING BRAVE THOUGH. AT THIS POINT, IT WAS FUCKING MASSIVE. THAT'S RIGHT, DORMICE ARE THE SIZE OF MOTHERFUCKING MOUNTAINS IN THIS PERIOD. IT RUNS UP TO THE SUN AND BEGINS TO BITE THROUGH THE NET, BUT THE HEAT IS TOO MUCH AND THE POOR DORMOUSE BEGINS TO SHRIVEL UP. IT TAKES FUCKING AGES TO BITE THROUGH ENOUGH OF THE NET FOR THE SUN TO ESCAPE AND RISE PROPERLY, AND BY THE TIME THE JOB IS FINISHED, THE DORMOUSE IS FUCKING TINY. IT'S FUCKING TRAGIC.

BEOWULF

BEOWULF MURDERS A MONSTER

HROTHGAR, KING OF THE DANES, LIKES TO PARTY. HE PARTIES ALL THE TIME. REALLY FUCKING LOUDLY. UNFORTUNATELY, THE LOCAL MONSTER DOESN'T LIKE TO PARTY. GRENDEL, A HUGE FUCKING MONSTER, JUST GETS PISSED OFF AT ALL THE NOISE. AND WHEN YOU PISS OFF A MONSTER, THINGS GET PRETTY FUCKING MESSY. EVERY NIGHT, GRENDEL SNEAKS INTO HIS HOUSE AND EATS ONE OF HIS MEN. THAT'S PRETTY FUCKING SHITTY. HE'S RUNNING OUT OF MEN, AND EVERY TIME HE GETS MORE, THE FUCKING MONSTER EATS THEM ALL.

ONE DAY, BEOWULF SHOWS UP. BEOWULF IS JUST SOME GUY THAT LIKES TO KILL MONSTERS. BEOWULF IS ALSO A COCKY LITTLE SHIT. HE DECIDES TO KILL THE MONSTER, BUT WITHOUT USING WEAPONS BECAUSE THAT WOULD BE TOO EASY. WHAT A DICK.

GRENDEL SHOWS UP TO EAT PEOPLE, BUT BEOWULF IS WAITING UP FOR HIM. BEOWULF SHOUTS "HA, GOT YOU, MOTHERFUCKER!" AND DIVES ON HIM. THEN HE WRESTLES THE GIANT MAN-EATING MONSTER. THEY WRESTLE SO MUCH THAT THE HALL FALLS DOWN. THEN BEOWULF TEARS OFF GRENDEL'S ARM WITH HIS BARE HANDS AND GOES BACK TO BED. GRENDEL CRAWLS HOME TO THE MARSHES AND BLEEDS TO DEATH.

ALL HE WANTED WAS A BIT OF SLEEP AND A BREAK FROM HROTHGAR'S ALL NIGHT PARTYING.

BEOWULF MURDERS A MONSTER'S MUM

AFTER MURDERING GRENDEL OVER A NOISE COMPLAINT, BEOWULF ISN'T HAPPY YET. HE WANTS TO KILL MORE INNOCENT MONSTERS. HE NAILS GRENDEL'S ARM TO THE WALL, AND THEN SETS OFF TO FIND SOMETHING ELSE TO MURDER. BEOWULF, LIKE ALL HEROES, IS A FUCKING DICK.

AFTER GRENDEL'S MUM SHOWS UP IN THE MIDDLE OF THE NIGHT TO AVENGE HER SON'S BRUTAL MURDER, BEOWULF FOLLOWS HER HOME. NOT ONLY IS HE A DICK, HE'S ONE CREEPY MOTHERFUCKER. GRENDEL'S MUM LIVES IN A CAVE AT THE BOTTOM OF A LAKE. BEOWULF, WEARING FULL ARMOUR AND CARRYING A SWORD, DIVES INTO THE LAKE TO KILL HER. SHE'S JUST A HARMLESS OLD LADY. WITH FANGS AND MUSCLES LIKE A BODYBUILDER AND GILLS AND A TENDENCY TO EAT PEOPLE.

TURNS OUT GRENDEL'S MUM IS IMMUNE TO SWORDS. BEOWULF THROWS AWAY HIS SWORD AND WRESTLES A LITTLE OLD LADY. THEN HE FINDS A MAGIC SWORD IN HER CAVE AND CUTS OFF HER HEAD. BEOWULF JUST REALLY LIKES KILLING THINGS, OK?

BEOWULF GETS HIS JUST DESSERTS

BEOWULF, RENOWNED MURDERER OF OLD LADIES, HAS RETIRED WITH A MASSIVE HEAP OF MOTHERFUCKING TREASURE. HE'S KING OF SOMEWHERE AND EVERYONE LOVES HIM BECAUSE HE KILLS FUCKING MONSTERS.

ONE DAY, ONE OF HIS MEN STEALS A GOLDEN CUP. FROM A MOTHERFUCKING DRAGON. THE DRAGON SHOWS UP AT BEOWULF'S HOUSE, TAKES THE CUP BACK AND SETS FIRE TO EVERYTHING. THIS IS ALL THE EXCUSE THAT BEOWULF (NOW AN OLD MAN BUT STILL A MURDERER) NEEDS TO FETCH HIS SWORD AND GO KILL THINGS.

HE SETS OFF TO MURDER THE DRAGON, BUT THIS IS A FUCKING DRAGON NOT SOME OLD LADY. THEY FIGHT FOR AGES, BUT BEOWULF DOESN'T STAND A FUCKING CHANCE. ALL HIS MEN, SEEING THAT HE NEEDS HELP, FUCK OFF AND ABANDON HIM.

ALL EXCEPT ONE. WIGLAF, HIS BEST FRIEND, GRABS A SWORD AND JOINS IN. BETWEEN THE TWO OF THEM, THEY MURDER THE DRAGON AND STEAL ALL ITS FUCKING GOLD. BEOWULF, HOWEVER, HAS BEEN MORTALLY WOUNDED IN THE FIGHT AND DIES SHORTLY AFTERWARDS.

WHAT A FUCKING ANTICLIMAX.

MORE MYTHS CAN BE FOUND AT
WWW.OEDIPUSMOTHERFUCKINGTYRANNUS.TUMBLR.COM

THE RT. HON. DR. NEMESIS R.M. LIGHTSLAYER THE MAGNIFICENT, BREAKER OF SPINES, TWEAKER OF UNMENTIONABLES IS A LARGE AND ANGRY DRAGON WITH TWO FUCKING HEADS AND FUCKING ENORMOUS POINTY TEETH. THEY WERE TRAGICALLY ORPHANED AS A CHILD IN A FUCKING HORRIFIC INCIDENT INVOLVING A BEAR AND A BUCKET OF BLUE PAINT. THE LOGICAL CONCLUSION OF THIS WAS THE DEDICATION OF THEIR LIFE TO A CAREER OF MOTHERFUCKING MYTHOLOGY, SHOUTING AND BEES.

DR. LIGHTSLAYER'S CAREER IN ACADEMIA IS SOMEWHAT MARRED BY THEIR INABILITY TO USE DOORS AND TYPE WITH EASE. THIS HAS NOT STOPPED THEM FROM TRYING AS HARD AS THEY FUCKING CAN, AND, AFTER COMPLETING A SERIES OF POSTGRADUATE COURSES IN INVECTIVE, THEY ARE NOW AN UNEXPECTEDLY SUCCESSFUL ACADEMIC AND BLOGGER.

DR. LIGHTSLAYER CURRENTLY LIVES IN A FUCKING MAGNIFICENT CAVE FULL OF GOLD SOMEWHERE IN ENGLAND, WHERE THEY CAN BE FOUND SCREAMING ABUSE AT ANYONE FOOLISH ENOUGH TO APPROACH THEIR FUCKING MAJESTY.

Made in the USA
San Bernardino, CA
18 June 2016